CONTENTS

Horse riding – and horse ownership – is becoming more popular every year, but it is not like other hobbies, where the equipment can be put away and forgotten when you have finished with it. The horse, or pony, needs constant, daily care and attention to keep him happy, fit and healthy. Just what does that involve?

Many new horse owners are bewildered by the deluge of conflicting advice they receive from different sources. In particular, modern research has shown that some of the accepted 'traditional' practices may not be the best methods to use, in the light of new knowledge and understanding.

The intention of this book is to provide a clear, straightforward and informed guide to modern horse ownership and care for those without previous experience, as much for the novice adult as for the enthusiastic young pony owner.

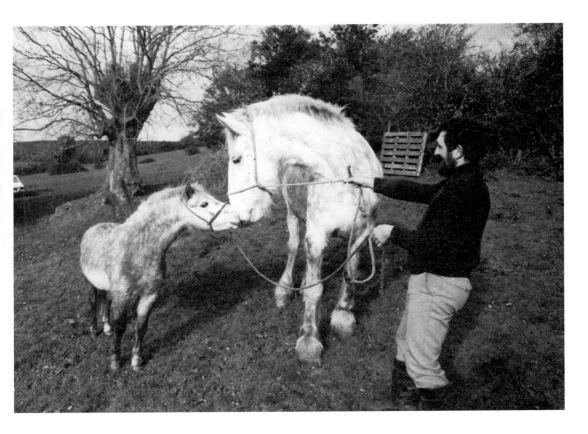

Buying your first horse or pony is perhaps one of the most exciting events in a lifetime of involvement with horses. After all the pleasurable anticipation this could be the start of a happy and lasting partnership, with memorable moments collected along the way. What can go wrong? And how can you avoid disappointment?

Sometimes the desire for a horse or pony 'of my own' takes precedence over regard for the welfare of the animal himself, with the result that horses and ponies are found living in quite unsuitable conditions, even on completely unsuitable food. Even a small pony needs ample room for exercise and the right kind of nutritious food. A shed at the bottom of the garden is by no means sufficient. Like all animals, horses and ponies are living creatures and although they cannot speak up for themselves, they need and deserve proper attention to their natural needs, including their mental, as well as their physical, health. Mental well-being is often ignored, even by quite experienced horse owners.

Points of the horse.

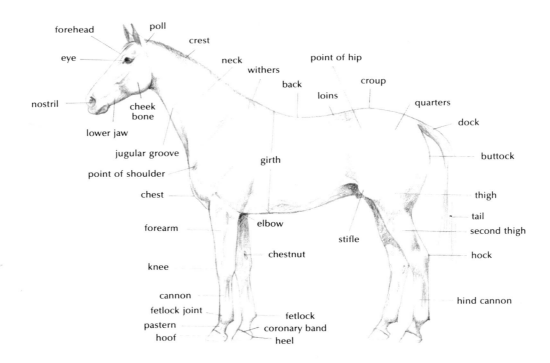

forehead poll crest
eye neck point of hip
withers back croup
nostril loins
cheek bone quarters
lower jaw dock
jugular groove girth buttock
point of shoulder thigh
chest tail
forearm elbow second thigh
stifle hock
chestnut
knee
cannon hind cannon
fetlock joint fetlock
pastern coronary band
hoof heel

Remember that equine ownership is a long term commitment. Of course you might want to sell on a younger horse or pony who has been outgrown, or who is not capable of reaching the equestrian heights to which you aspire, in which case your only responsibility is to see that he goes to a caring and knowledgeable home. Sometimes, good homes can be found where the animal can carry on with 'light' work, but retired horses and ponies still need good food, shelter, fresh water and routine health care. Congenial company is very important, since he will seldom leave his field and solitary horses or ponies are unhappy creatures.

An undernourished youngster. Note the prominent ribs and lack of flesh over the withers, loins and quarters. This young horse will never reach his full potential unless quick action is taken to improve his condition.

If you cannot find your old horse or pony a suitable retirement home and do not have the facilities or resources to keep him happily in retirement yourself, you should consider that the difficult decision be taken to put him down. This can be done quickly and humanely in his own yard or paddock, or at a licensed abattoir and you will have the peace of mind of knowing that you did your best for him to the end. Sending him to a sale just causes unnecessary bewilderment and possible suffering and simply shifts the responsibility for disposing of him on to someone else.

In choosing a horse or pony, the rider's size, weight and ability must be considered. The rider on the left in this photograph appears too tall for her mount. Although he looks sturdy and capable of carrying her weight, she would be more comfortable on a taller horse. The rider in the centre has a nice position and her horse looks a kind, dependable sort, but she would find it easier to balance herself and apply the aids on a smaller horse. The rider on the right is correctly mounted for her weight and size.

If you are going to pay a sensible price for a mount and thus commit yourself to the not inconsiderable cost of looking after him (providing stabling, grazing, feed and bedding, paying for the outlay on necessary equipment, veterinary fees and farriery charges) it makes sense to be absolutely certain that the horse you buy will suit you.

The first thing to consider is your own experience and, if this is going to be the first horse you actually own, your experience is unlikely to be very great. Perhaps you have had some riding lessons, or helped out at someone else's stables or yard? If you have actually worked with horses, of course you are at an advantage, but it is essential only to buy a horse or pony you can handle with confidence, both in the saddle and on the ground. This may seem to be obvious advice, but it is extra-

ordinary how many owners quickly become disillusioned, when they find that, for one reason or another, they cannot cope with the animals they have bought. Looking after your pony is all important. Apart from your horse or pony's own welfare, you will want to keep him in the right condition to be able to carry out his workload particularly if you want to show, hunt or take part in competitive events and you will have disappointing results if your mount is not in a fit and healthy condition.

Beginners frequently make the mistake of buying a horse who is either too big, or too highly bred. If you remember that the horse and rider should be in harmony with one another, it is easy to understand why a small or slight rider might have difficulties coping with a large, big-striding horse. The highly bred horse has lightning-quick reactions and needs the skills of an experienced rider and handler to manage him efficiently.

So your initial aim should be to look for a horse or pony who is the right size and has the right temperament. Size should be considered in terms of build (both your own and that of the horse) and substance or weight, as well as height. Adults of less than slender build often make the error of choosing a rotund, cobby type of horse, giving themselves unnecessary difficulty in acquiring a deep seat. The selected mount must have sufficient bone to carry the required weight, but this can be found in horses of good riding conformation as easily as in those inclined to stoutness. Look for good native pony crosses who have then been crossed with Thoroughbreds.

A tall person obviously needs a taller horse than a shorter person, but again, take care not to over-horse yourself in the quest for a leggy mount, since these tend to have a high proportion of 'hot' Thoroughbred blood. If a tall horse is needed, an Irish Draught cross, or a Warmblood, will usually have an equable temperament.

A pony bought for a child should be bought with the child's growth rate in mind and, obviously, a younger child will need changes of mount as he or she grows up. Good children's ponies can usually be sold on to good homes for the benefit of other, younger generations of riders, so do not make the mistake of buying a pony that is too big for a child to cope with easily at the start. Too large or strong a mount will quickly frighten a child beginner and destroy his confidence.

When choosing a Horse or Pony you should consider:

1. Rider
   Experience
   Height and weight
   Riding aims
2. Horse or Pony
   Breed
   Age
   Type/build
   Temperament
   Soundness
   Fitness for
     intended use
   Level of training/
     experience
   Competition
     record

Early Lessons should include some or all of the following:

1. Grooming
2. Tacking up
3. Mounting and dismounting
4. A good position
5. Balance at walk and trot
6. Use of the aids
7. Untacking

How do we define a good 'temperament'? To the beginner, it means a horse or pony who can be handled easily, who is willing and obedient and will not be easily upset. Therefore the horse's early life and training comes into the equation, as well as his innate character. A horse or pony who has been correctly and sympathetically cared for and schooled during his formative years should cause the first time owner few problems. One who has been mistreated, or badly broken or schooled, however, could cause you much heartache. The best buy, therefore, for a new horse or pony owner, is one recommended by a trusted friend or other knowledgeable person, or even better, one who is already known to you. Riding schools and livery yards often have horses or ponies for sale and it is worthwhile getting to know your local establishments before you think of buying. In that way you might have the opportunity to get to know your future mount and perhaps ride him regularly, to make sure you are suited, before you commit yourself to the purchase.

Many people cherish the dream of 'a horse of my own' for years before the opportunity to make it a reality arises. But it is not a good idea to buy a horse or pony before you have some experience of riding and horse care. Riding requires skills that cannot be learned as easily as signing the cheque to buy your horse, whilst keeping your own horse or pony at home entails the commitment to attend to his needs at least twice a day, seven days a week, or if you cannot do this yourself, to make appropriate arrangements for someone to do it for you. Learn what is involved before you buy, spend time at a riding school and invest some money in riding lessons at a reputable centre. That way you will be prepared to give your mount the best care and will avoid taking unnecessary risks when riding.

Some lessons before you buy your first horse or pony, and with him once he arrives, can save many problems.

AGE

Others matters also need to be weighed up when considering the purchase of a suitable horse or pony. For example, a beginner's mount must be old enough to have completed his basic training and then been ridden on until he is settled and

Skilled attention every four to six weeks is essential to keep your horse or pony's feet in good condition, so book a regular call from your farrier.

well mannered in all that is asked of him. This means looking for an animal of at least six or seven years of age. However, if you want to have years of fun and useful work from him he should not be too old, ideally no more than ten or eleven. On the other hand, if a mount is required for a particularly nervous person, an older, quieter horse should be considered.

CONFORMATION

It is also important to look for the type of horse that is going to be suitable for the work you want him to do. If you want to show, conformation is important. If show-jumping is your aim, you will want a short coupled, muscular horse, with strong, clean legs and scope at the shoulder. Each different horse sport requires a particular type of animal for success. However, for a general purpose horse or pony, with whom you can have a lot of fun, aim for the right size, build, temperament and age, with as good conformation as you can find.

LEGAL MATTERS

Finally, a word on the legal aspects of horse or pony owner-ship. At present there is no statutory requirement to insure your horse and you are entitled to use public highways without the payment of any road tax, unlike motor vehicles. However, in the event of an accident involving your horse, you might be held responsible in the same way as a car driver. It is therefore very sensible to take out public liability insurance, which is inexpensive and will cover you against liability for damage to other persons and their property. You can also, if you wish, insure your horse against death, loss of use, theft, theft of tack, veterinary fees and various other losses. Many policies are available and the most important advice is to read the 'small print' before signing anything, to be sure that you are insuring exactly what you wish to.

Unfortunately, in this age of ever increasing building and urbanization, riding on public roads is often unavoidable. It is also dangerous, so equip yourself with an up-to-date know-ledge of the Highway Code and read the British Horse Society's publication on riding and road safety.

Riding Safely:

1. Wear an approved safety helmet
2. Check tack regularly for wear and tear
3. Wear safe footwear
4. Take the BHS Riding and Road Safety test
5. Follow the Highway Code

Most part-bred or native horses and ponies can live outdoors most of the time, although a stable is needed for emergencies, and for convenience for visits from your vet or farrier, or for grooming and tacking up.

Even stabled horses who are in full work need to be turned out for at least an hour or two every day, and so access to suitable grazing is essential. It is really unrealistic to consider keeping a horse or pony unless you have at least 1.5 to 2 acres available for grazing. This should ideally be divided into two paddocks. For more animals, the grazing needs to be increased proportionately. Many owners do manage to keep a horse or pony on a smaller area, but if you are obliged to do this, good pasture management is all the more vital. You should also try to find some alternative pasture to rent for a few weeks, say twice a year, to give your horse or pony a holiday and his home field a rest.

Overgrazing your pasture results in several problems. In summer, the grass is frequently eaten down until the ground is bare, but weeds remain untouched and flourish. If action is not taken, they will take over the land entirely, choking off the

The red worm life cycle.

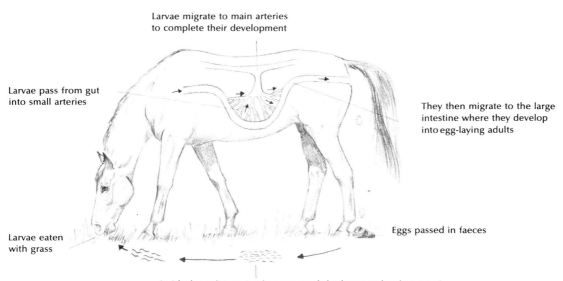

Larvae migrate to main arteries
to complete their development

Larvae pass from gut
into small arteries

They then migrate to the large
intestine where they develop
into egg-laying adults

Eggs passed in faeces

Larvae eaten
with grass

In ideal conditions it takes one week for larvae to hatch out and
develop into infective larvae

grass. Parasitic worms also flourish when droppings are left in pasture grazed exclusively by horses, since there is no break in their life cycle. Finally, in winter, wet ground becomes badly poached, leaving the horse or pony standing in inches of mud. The vicious circle is completed in the spring, when the land takes longer to recover and generate new grass.

PARASITIC WORMS

Large Strongyle (*Strongylus vulgaris, Strongylus edentatus* and *Strongylus equinus*)
Appearance: Thin worm 1–5cm long; reddish black in colour.
Infestation: All horses, from point where they start to pick up the larvae from the pasture.
Life cycle/Activity: Up to six months, commencing when larvae are taken in with food from the pasture and reach the small intestine. Damage is caused by the larvae migrating through the arteries, back to the small intestine, and eventually to the large intestine, where they mature and cause further damage, whilst also producing new eggs, which are passed out by the horse with the droppings. Symptoms of heavy infestation and damage may include colic (especially in young horses), gradual loss of condition and anaemia.

Small Strongyle (*Trichonema*)
Appearance: Similar to Large Strongyle but smaller.
Infestation: All horses.
Life cycle: Similar to Large Strongyle, but remains in small intestine until larvae emerge, often in early spring. Large infestations result in acute diarrhoea, which may be fatal.

Pinworm (*Oxyuris equi*)
Appearance: Eggs show up as grey/yellow streaks around anus.
Infestation: Common in young horses.
Life cycle/Activity: Causes intense irritation by laying eggs around anus.

Whiteworm or Ascarid (*Parascaris equorum*)
Appearance: Thick worm, up to 50cm long.
Infestation: Mainly foals from three months of age and young horses up to three years.
Life cycle/Activity: Eggs are picked up from the pasture and larvae migrate from the intestine via the liver to the lungs. They are coughed up, reswallowed and return to the intestine where they mature and produce eggs. A heavy burden causes unthriftiness and occasionally a blocked or ruptured intestine.

Bots (*Gastrophilus*)
Appearance: Reddish brown segmented larvae 1cm long.
Infestation: All horses.
Life Cycle/Activity: This is not a worm, but the larvae of the bot fly. The fly annoys horses between July and September, when it lays a mass of yellow eggs which are clearly visible on the coat. The larvae attach themselves to the stomach wall where they remain until spring when they are passed out with the droppings to mature into flies.

Note: Horses and ponies should be regularly dosed with a suitable worming preparation, every four to six weeks during summer and slightly less frequently in winter, at which time a preparation which is effective against bots should be used.

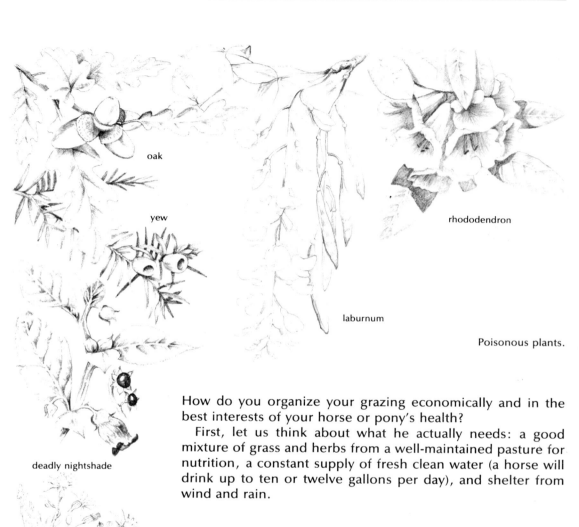

oak

yew

rhododendron

laburnum

Poisonous plants.

deadly nightshade

ragwort

How do you organize your grazing economically and in the best interests of your horse or pony's health?

First, let us think about what he actually needs: a good mixture of grass and herbs from a well-maintained pasture for nutrition, a constant supply of fresh clean water (a horse will drink up to ten or twelve gallons per day), and shelter from wind and rain.

GRAZING

Good grass growth is ensured by harrowing out old growth, rolling, re-seeding as necessary and applying an appropriate fertilizer – organic or artificial, but ask your local merchant for advice – at the appropriate times of the year.

A good mixture of field grasses will include perennial rye-grass, timothy, fescue, cocksfoot and a limited amount of clover. Weeds, such as docks and thistles, need to be topped before they seed.

RAGWORT

Is a poisonous plant particularly dangerous to horses and should be pulled by hand and burned. Horses are more likely to eat it when it is wilted, so never leave pulled ragwort lying around. It can also find its way into hay, which is another reason for only buying good quality fodder.

Good pasture management means a healthy horse in a safe environment. Rolling counteracts the effects of poaching and firms up the soil, encouraging good grass growth on reseeded ground. Also notice the neat hedge and safe fencing.

WATER SUPPLY

Your water supply can be natural, from a flowing stream or spring, or piped to a trough. Troughs must be cleaned out regularly and drinking places at springs or streams must be deep enough to ensure that the horse does not suck in sand with the water.

SHELTER

Shelter can be provided in several ways. A thick hedge is the best windbreak and horses will usually prefer to stand under a hedge, with their backs to the rain, rather than go into a man-made field shelter. A hollow in the lie of the land may also sometimes be a favoured spot, out of the wind, whilst trees will give shade from the sun in summer. See that any low branches are cut back safely. Fences should be strong and secure, gaps in fences and hedges should be properly repaired for safety and loose or sagging wire must be avoided at all costs. Post and wire fencing may sometimes be unavoidable, but the wire should be adequately strained and it helps if you can place rails along the top, both to avoid horses leaning on the wire and to make the fencing more visible from a distance.

PASTURE MAINTENANCE

However small your pasture, try to have it divided into two, so that each section can be grazed in rotation. This gives you the opportunity in spring or autumn to tidy up the unused area, re-

A combination fence of post, rail and wire, suitable for horses, but notice how the top rail has been chewed. This can be discouraged by regular creosote treatments.

seed or fertilize, as necessary. Never restock newly fertilized pasture until all the chemicals have been well washed into the ground by rain.

Sheep or cattle which graze ground after horses will help fertilize the land and will also break the life cycle of worms. Removing horse droppings once or twice a week will go a long way towards preventing eggs and larvae being consumed by grazing horses and ponies. Harrowing will also break up the moist faeces in which the eggs survive and will expose them to be killed by the heat of the sun in summer.

Two ways of maintaining good grazing are to divide your available pasture into at least two sections and graze alternately, or to combine grazing horses and ponies with other livestock, such as sheep or cattle.

Your stable need not be lavish, provided it meets the basic requirements to keep your horse or pony in good health. Being shut up for long hours in an inadequate building can considerably damage a horse's health, condition and, ultimately, his competitive ability.

A stable needs to be big enough for the horse or pony to turn round, roll and lie down in comfort, to be dry and free from draughts, and to be well ventilated. Most ponies can be accommodated in a box 10×10ft (3×3m), whilst a generous size for a large horse would be 14×12ft (4.2×3.5m). A good compromise, if you are building new stables, is 12×10–12ft (3.5×3–3.5m) for average sized horses.

To keep a stable dry, it needs to drain well, which means the floor should have a slight slope (or fall) in the direction of the drainage outlet. Stables which are not well drained soon start to smell of ammonia, from collected pools of urine.

An example of efficient, modern, purpose-built stabling. Notice the windows protected by wire mesh and the ventilation hoppers on the roof.

A traditional stone building has been adapted with brick additions to form a stable. The door opening is too low for a horse of this size, whereas a pony might be comfortably accommodated.

Draughts usually get in under badly fitting doors, so get these attended to before your new horse or pony arrives. Finally, ventilation is not usually a problem in purpose built stabling, if air inlets are provided at low level, with high level outlets. Traditional stables may need some attention to improve the ventilation system, which should be adequate enough to prevent the horse breathing in an atmosphere polluted with mould spores and dust from hay and straw.

Many traditional stone or brick built livestock buildings are suitable for conversion to use as stabling, or modern purpose built stables can be constructed in blockwork, or timber. Under current British legislation, the provision of stables requires planning consent from your local planning authority. In the United States check your local zoning ordinance.

In your stable you will need a manger, or frame into which a feed bucket can be placed, a similar holder for a water bucket, and a hay rack, or a secure ring to attach a hay net.

Bedding can be straw, woodshavings, shredded paper or peat and we will look more closely at these on pages 48–9.

Feeding your horse or pony need not be a complicated business, even at competitive level. He needs roughage, or 'bulk' food, plus 'concentrates' or energy giving food. Bulk food includes grass, hay, ensiled hay and grass, straw, chaff, sugar beet pulp, lucerne (alfalfa), succulents such as carrots and apples and bran. Concentrates include cereals such as oats, barley and maize, plus peas and beans, oil, linseed, molasses, milk products and compound feeds.

All horses and ponies need an adequate, preferably ad lib supply of basic roughage at all times, whilst concentrate food

---

SAMPLE DIET SHEETS

A. 15.2hh riding horse, bodyweight approx 500kg.
Total requirement = 2.5 per cent bodyweight. Therefore 2.5 per cent × 500 = 12.5kg per day.

1. *Resting*: 12.5kg grass and/or good quality hay. In winter a small proportion of concentrate feed should be given to provide extra energy for warmth. Increase or decrease concentrates according to condition. Hay should be fed preferably ad lib, since there is no danger of over-feeding hay.
2. *Light Work* (i.e. hacking): Good grass may be sufficient in summer. From August, as grass deteriorates, commence feeding hay. Concentrates should be fed according to workload and condition, but for light work should not need to exceed 25 per cent of total food requirement.
3. *Medium/hard work* (i.e. hunting, riding club, jumping): Up to 50 per cent of diet may be required as concentrates, i.e. a maximum of 6kg divided into at least three feeds, plus 6.5kg hay. If horse can be turned out to graze during the day, proportionately less hay will be needed and the hay net can be provided at night.
4. *High Performance Work* (i.e. racing, endurance work, three-day eventing): Up to 75 per cent of the diet may be required as concentrates. At this level the horse's diet needs expert management to correctly balance the essential nutrient requirements and the details are beyond the scope of this book.

B. 13.2hh pony, bodyweight approx 300kg.
Total requirement: 2.5 per cent × 300 = 7.5kg per day.

1. *Resting*: Grass/hay according to time of year. More highly bred ponies will need a proportion of their diet fed as concentrates in winter, for energy and warmth, whereas native breeds will usually require only hay.
2. *Light work* (i.e. hacking, mainly at weekends). As for resting, but up to 25 per cent concentrates in winter, according to breed/hardiness.
3. *Medium/hard work* (i.e. hunting, Pony Club, jumping): Up to 50 per cent of diet can be fed as concentrates, e.g. 3.5kg horse and pony cubes in at least two feeds, plus 4kg grass/hay. Ponies turned out in summer must not be allowed to become too fat. Restrict grazing if necessary.

should be provided in accordance with the horse's breed, type, age, size and workload. With so many variable factors, it is impossible to lay down exact rules for quantities and although as a rough guide, a horse will eat about 2.5 per cent of his bodyweight each day, the best guide for a conscientious owner is observation of the horse's condition, coupled with common sense. (*See* opposite for sample diet sheets for a working 15.2hh. riding horse, and a working 13.2hh. pony.) Horses at rest need less food than those in work, although all but the hardiest native ponies will need some concentrates during the winter months. Breeding mares and youngstock need a slightly higher level of protein than other animals.

Examples of an overweight and an underweight pony.

How do you know if your horse or pony is getting enough food? First, note whether he looks healthy, with a shining coat and bright, alert eyes and whether he has a good covering of flesh. This does not mean he should be fat, and overfeeding can cause more serious problems than underfeeding. To be in good condition, his ribs should be covered and his loins should be flat, not falling away, when you lay your hand across them. His skin should be elastic, not taut and stretched, and move easily under your fingers. An overfed, obese horse will have a large gut, ripples of fat over his shoulders and, often, a heavily crested neck. A horse who is too thin will have tight, stretched skin, with all his ribs visible and prominent hip bones, and the loins and quarters falling away.

It is not usually necessary to feed hay in summer when there is ample grass growing, unless your grazing is very limited and your horse or pony spends the major part of his time in the stable. Many ponies are inclined to get fat very quickly and need little if any concentrate food, unless they are working very hard. Special care must be taken when the first flush of spring grass (and later the second flush of summer growth)

A cut down plastic barrel makes a convenient water butt for the stable yard.

occurs, to see that these ponies do not rapidly become over-weight and succumb to laminitis (*see* page 80).

BULK FEED

Straw is rarely fed, except in chaff, or sometimes in conjunction with silage, but if your horse takes a fancy to good oat straw it will do him no harm. However, it is very important to prevent horses from eating dusty straw, or an allergic reaction will almost certainly develop. Unfortunately, old fashioned long oat straw is hard to come by, most nowadays being the short, dusty product of combine harvesting.

Ensiled hay, sold in various proprietary forms, has become popular in recent years and does help provide a dust-free diet, if fed in accordance with the maker's recommendations.

In Britain, chaff and soaked sugar beet pulp both make excellent mixers to prevent horses from bolting their hard feed. Sugar beet pulp must be soaked for at least twelve hours in hot water or twenty-four hours in cold water, before feeding. It is particularly useful in having a slightly laxative effect for stabled horses on a basically dry diet, and is high in calcium, which helps to counteract the lack of this important mineral in a cereal-based diet. It is also very palatable and thus is useful in encouraging a shy feeder to eat.

Lucerne, known as alfalfa in the States, can be fed fresh, as hay, ensiled hay or as proprietary nuts and is increasingly popular for competition horses and breeding stock. Care should be taken to reduce as appropriate the amount of concentrates fed with lucerne, as it is high in protein.

TITBITS

Succulents (apples, carrots and other root crops) are much appreciated by horses and make tempting additions to give variety to feeds for stabled animals.

CONCENTRATES

For feeding concentrates there are two alternative approaches. You can either mix your own ration, from cereals and other

hay

sugar beet pulp and nuts

mollichaff

succulents

maize

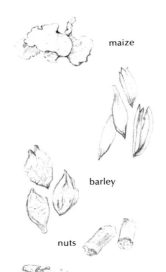

barley

nuts

mix

ingredients mentioned above, or, if you are not sufficiently confident to do this, use proprietary compound feeds in the form of horse and pony nuts or coarse mixes. These are available in numerous formulations designed to meet the requirements of every different type of equine from the high-performance competition horse to the infrequently exercised hack, so it is merely a matter of shopping around for the most suitable brand and compound. (*See* below for a chart of foodstuffs.) How your horse or pony's diet requirements might vary during the year, will be considered on pages 22–3.

FEEDS AND THEIR USES

Bulk Foods (Roughage or fibre)
Grass: Well maintained meadow pasture, containing a good mixture of grasses and herbs, provides all the necessary nutrients for a healthy horse or pony, subject to soil variations and the changing seasons.
Hay: Made from dried grass, provides main nutrient requirements according to quality. Good quality hay is cut at the correct stage of growth and saved quickly in fine weather. Seed hay has a higher protein content than meadow hay and is usually fed to working horses. Hay is of less nutritional value than grass and may be deficient in vitamins.
Ensiled hay: Sold in proprietary form specially made for horses, this is excellent for horses needing a dust-free environment and is of higher nutritional value than ordinary hay, so proportionately less concentrates are needed.
Chaff: Chopped hay and good quality oat straw, mixed together to form a mixer for concentrate feed, to provide bulk and prevent gobbling.
Sugar Beet Pulp: A highly palatable bulk food, which helps put on condition. Ideal as a mixer for concentrates and relatively high in calcium. *Sugar beet pulp must be soaked for 24 hours in cold water (12 hours in hot water) before feeding.* Unsoaked sugar beet will cause a digestive upset that may prove fatal, so store opened bags in a sealed container, inaccessible to horses.
Alfalfa (Lucerne): High protein food, also high in calcium, often fed to breeding stock or high performance horses. Can be fed fresh, is made into hay (in USA), or is available chopped and baled or as proprietary nuts.
Extruded feed: Currently popular method of providing a greater proportion of the diet as easily digested carbohydrate, achieved by a special cooking process called 'extrusion'. Applicable only to high performance horses and must be fed as part of a balanced diet.
Bran: Traditionally used as a mixer, but now inadvisable due to difficulty in obtaining good quality broad bran and imbalance in calcium/phosphorus ratio required by horse. May be used in form of bran mash if purgative is required, but this is also inadvisable in normal circumstances, since horse's digestive system does not cope well with sudden changes.
Succulents: (e.g. carrots and apples) Excellent for tempting poor appetites when added to the feed. Must be sliced lengthways to avoid risk of choking.

Concentrates (High energy foods)
Proprietary compound feeds: Available as cubes or coarse mixes and formulated according to use and workload of horse. Compound feeds should not be mixed with 'straights' (i.e. other concentrates) and care should be taken as regards additional vitamin and mineral supplementation, since most compounds are already balanced with a broad spectrum of essential vitamins and minerals. Convenient method of feeding for those not wishing to cope with balancing a diet of 'straights' and supplements.
Oats: Traditionally fed to horses because of easy digestibility compared with other cereals. Comparatively high in fibre and low in calcium. Good quality oats are increasingly difficult to obtain, so alternatives are becoming more popular.
Barley: Cooking improves digestibility. Excellent for putting on condition.
Maize/corn: High carbohydrate content and fed in small amounts to add condition and tempt fussy feeders. May be fed on cob, shelled or flaked.
Vegetable oil: Used to increase fat content of diet for high performance horses. Must be carefully balanced with other rations and is of value only when a high level of fitness has been achieved.
Linseed: Poisonous raw, but traditionally boiled to make jelly and fed to improve coat condition of show horses.
Milk: Usually fed in powder or pellet form, to youngstock, brood mares and convalescent horses to help build up condition.
Molasses: Derivative of sugar used to tempt appetite and also used in some proprietary feeds to reduce dust and improve palatability, e.g. molassed chaff.

Vitamins and Minerals
The essential vitamin and mineral requirements of most horses should be found in good quality feed and forage and supplementation should not be necessary. However, if the feed quality is suspect, a good broad spectrum supplement can be added at the manufacturer's recommended dosage rates. Most vitamins are toxic if overfed, so do not exceed basic requirements. The most important vitamins and minerals are:
Vitamin A for healthy bones, joints, mucous membranes and good eyesight.
Vitamin B Group:
  Folic Acid – for healthy red blood cells.
  Biotin and Methionate – for hoof and hair growth.
  Thiamine – for energy production. Bracken poisoning causes thiamine deficiency.
Vitamin D for the regulation of calcium and phosphorus absorption by the body.
Vitamin E for healthy muscle development.
Vitamin K for blood clotting; but overdosing more common than deficiency.
Calcium for healthy bone growth.
Phosphorus for healthy bone growth.
Magnesium for efficient functioning of the nervous system.
Trace Elements: (Supplementation not required unless a specific deficiency is diagnosed).
  Copper – for growth.
  Cobalt – for growth.
  Selenium – required with Vitamin E for muscle development.
  Zinc – contributes to healthy hoof formation.

Transactions concerning horses are often carried out without sufficient forethought. If you buy at an auction, you should check the conditions of sale to see if any warranty is being given that the horse is sound. If you buy privately, you will have little chance of getting your money back if the horse or pony should prove unsound, unless you have the terms of sale in writing from the vendor. In any event, except to the extent of any warranty given, it is the buyer's responsibility to satisfy him or herself that the animal is suitable. The vendor is not obliged to volunteer any information which might prejudice his sale.

It is in your own interest to have the horse or pony vetted by a qualified veterinary surgeon *before* you part with any money. Warranties are usually given at auction sales for forty-eight hours only, and usually provide only for the animal being sound in respiration (wind), limb and eye, so there is no right to a refund in respect of other problems.

A full veterinary examination might seem expensive at the time, but could well save you years of expense and heartache later. For valuable animals, X-rays of the feet might be taken to check for any signs of bone diseases.

The vet will check the horse or pony's heart as part of his purchase examination.

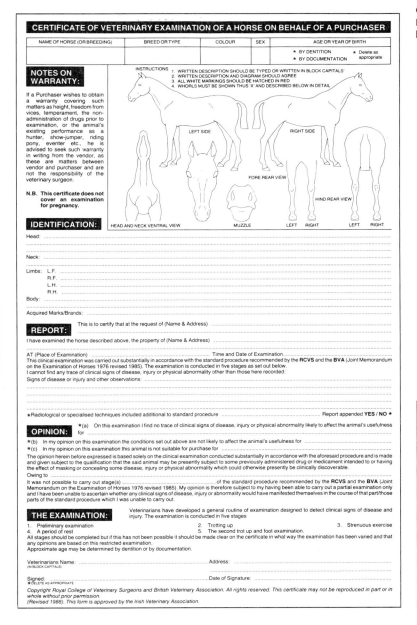

Certificate of Veterinary Examination of a horse on behalf of a purchaser.

CERTIFICATE OF VETERINARY EXAMINATION OF A HORSE ON BEHALF OF A PURCHASER

NAME OF HORSE (OR BREEDING)	BREED OR TYPE	COLOUR	SEX	AGE OR YEAR OF BIRTH
				★ BY DENTITION ★ Delete as appropriate ★ BY DOCUMENTATION

INSTRUCTIONS
1. WRITTEN DESCRIPTION SHOULD BE TYPED OR WRITTEN IN BLOCK CAPITALS'
2. WRITTEN DESCRIPTION AND DIAGRAM SHOULD AGREE
3. ALL WHITE MARKINGS SHOULD BE HATCHED IN RED
4. WHORLS MUST BE SHOWN THUS 'X' AND DESCRIBED BELOW IN DETAIL

LEFT SIDE RIGHT SIDE

FORE REAR VIEW

HIND REAR VIEW

HEAD AND NECK VENTRAL VIEW   MUZZLE   LEFT   RIGHT   LEFT   RIGHT

NOTES ON WARRANTY:

If a Purchaser wishes to obtain a warranty covering such matters as height, freedom from vices, temperament, the non-administration of drugs prior to examination, or the animal's existing performance as a hunter, show-jumper, riding pony, eventer etc., he is advised to seek such warranty in writing from the vendor, as these are matters between vendor and purchaser and are not the responsibility of the veterinary surgeon.

N.B. This certificate does not cover an examination for pregnancy.

IDENTIFICATION:

Head: ....

Neck: ....

Limbs: L.F. ....
R.F. ....
L.H. ....
R.H. ....

Body: ....

Acquired Marks/Brands: ....

REPORT:

This is to certify that at the request of (Name & Address) ....

I have examined the horse described above, the property of (Name & Address) ....

AT (Place of Examination) .... Time and Date of Examination ....
This clinical examination was carried out substantially in accordance with the standard procedure recommended by the **RCVS** and the **BVA** (Joint Memorandum on the Examination of Horses 1976 revised 1985). The examination is conducted in five stages as set out below.
I cannot find any trace of clinical signs of disease, injury or physical abnormality other than those here recorded:
Signs of disease or injury and other observations: ....

★Radiological or specialised techniques included additional to standard procedure .... Report appended **YES / NO** ★

OPINION:

★(a) On this examination I find no trace of clinical signs of disease, injury or physical abnormality likely to affect the animal's usefulness for ....

★(b) In my opinion on this examination the conditions set out above are not likely to affect the animal's usefulness for ....

★(c) In my opinion on this examination this animal is not suitable for purchase for ....

The opinion herein before expressed is based solely on the clinical examination conducted substantially in accordance with the aforesaid procedure and is made and given subject to the qualification that the said animal may be presently subject to some previously administered drug or medicament intended to or having the effect of masking or concealing some disease, injury or physical abnormality which could otherwise presently be clinically discoverable.

Owing to ....

It was not possible to carry out stage(s) ....of the standard procedure recommended by the **RCVS** and the **BVA** (Joint Memorandum on the Examination of Horses 1976 revised 1985). My opinion is therefore subject to my having been able to carry out a partial examination only and I have been unable to ascertain whether any clinical signs of disease, injury or abnormality would have manifested themselves in the course of that part/those parts of the standard procedure which I was unable to carry out.

THE EXAMINATION:

Veterinarians have developed a general routine of examination designed to detect clinical signs of disease and injury. The examination is conducted in five stages

1. Preliminary examination
2. Trotting up
3. Strenuous exercise
4. A period of rest
5. The second trot up and foot examination.

All stages should be completed but if this has not been possible it should be made clear on the certificate in what way the examination has been varied and that any opinions are based on this restricted examination.
Approximate age may be determined by dentition or by documentation.

Veterinarians Name: .... Address: ....
(IN BLOCK CAPITALS)

Signed: .... Date of Signature: ....
★DELETE AS APPROPRIATE.

The vet will examine the horse or pony's eyes, mouth and teeth, his limbs and feet, his general physical state of health, his heart, his wind and his action and will indicate whether, in his opinion, the animal is suitable for the purpose for which it is being bought (hacking, competitive work or showing).

Other potential problems must be resolved by trying the horse or pony out and questioning the vendor. At an auction sale you will not have the opportunity to ride your prospective purchase, but it might be possible to watch the owner show the horse or pony off. This is not a very satisfactory way for a beginner or first time owner to buy a horse, which is the reason why auctions are best left to the experts.

Buying privately, if you are lucky, you might be able to persuade the owner to let you have the horse or pony on trial, although most owners are reluctant to do this, for fear of mishaps. If this is not possible, make the most of the opportunity to try the animal out before you come to a decision. Take an experienced person with you, who will give you an unbiased opinion of the horse or pony's suitability and who can also witness the terms upon which you agree to buy.

Waiting to be sold – but the auction sale is not the place for a beginner to buy a horse or pony.

Don't be fobbed off with a ready tacked up animal and a quick ride down the lane and back. If the horse is at grass, ask that he be left in the field until you arrive, so you can see if he is easy to catch. Involve yourself in grooming him, pick up his feet and tack him up yourself, to discover if he is easy to handle. Expect to have a reasonable ride, away from and towards home, in traffic if possible and in a field where you can check his level of schooling. Hacking out will show you whether he is well-mannered and balanced, but you should also be able to ride straightforward school movements, such as circles and changes of rein. Include jumping, if that is part of your plans and ride the horse at walk, trot and canter. If an ability to gallop is important to your purposes, the horse should be galloped, with the owner's permission.

Points to look for:

1. Conformation
2. Action/paces
3. Health and condition
4. Clean limbs, free from blemishes
5. No vices
6. Right size and type
7. Good manners and temperament
8. Well schooled
9. Suitability for purpose

PAST HISTORY

Find out as much as you can about the horse or pony from his owner. Is he registered with a breed society or competitive organization? What is his breeding? What is his past performance record? Has he any wins or placings to his credit? Does he have a vaccination certificate and is it up to date?

Ask directly if he has ever suffered from any disease or injury that the owner is aware of, and whether he has ever been seen to display any 'vices'. Make notes of the answers given.

'Vices' include behavioural vices, such as biting, kicking or rearing and you will have obtained a good idea about the possibility of these whilst handling and riding the horse. Also included are so-called stable vices – crib biting, wind sucking and weaving. Any tendency to these indicates some problem in the horse's attitude towards his life (better management will sometimes cure them) and they will also adversely affect his physical health and condition.

If, having satisfied yourself on all these points, you still wish to buy the horse or pony, agree a price, subject to vetting and arrange for your vet to examine him as soon as possible. No vendor should object to his horse or pony being vetted, but it is also reasonable for him to continue to offer him for sale, until the price is paid. Once you have found the right animal, therefore, it is in your interests to complete the transaction without delay.

When your purchase arrives, you will no doubt be longing to try him out again, but the first priority is to settle him into his future home.

Once he is unloaded, first offer him a drink of fresh water, especially if he has come any distance. Remove his travelling boots or bandages and check him over for any minor injuries sustained on the journey. Walk him for a few minutes to let him relax and stretch his legs, before leading him into his stable, which should be prepared for him.

Check his rugs or blankets, if worn, changing them as necessary if he has sweated up whilst travelling and generally see that he is comfortable. Then leave him with a bucket of fresh, clean water and a small haynet, to settle down. Later, at a convenient time, he can have his usual feed – find out from the previous owner what food he is usually given and stick to the same if possible, until you get to know him better and can work out what he needs for yourself.

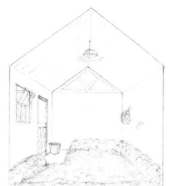

Later in the day, if he is sufficiently settled and not too tired (wait until the next day if he arrived in the afternoon), take him for a short, quiet ride and start getting to know him. Keep all your actions calm, firm and quiet and your aids sensitive and light. Aim always to continue in this way.

Soon after he arrives, it is advisable to give your new horse or pony a wormer. Make a note of the date and the type of preparation given, for future reference. Remember to worm him approximately every six weeks thereafter. Horses should be wormed slightly more frequently in summer, when worm activity is at its greatest, and less frequently in winter. Horses grazing together must all be wormed at the same time and the more horses there are grazing the available pasture, the more frequently they should be dosed. Do not turn your new arrival out in his field for forty-eight hours after worming, to give the dose time to take effect.

A horse arriving at his new home will need to rest after a long journey. This one is tacked up to travel in a quilted rug and leg bandages. The padding under the bandages descends over the heels for protection. For additional safety the horse could wear knee and hock boots, plus a poll guard attached to his headcollar.

Regular worming is essential – every four to six weeks – especially if your pasture is heavily grazed by horses. Worming preparations can be purchased from your vet and the drugs used should be alternated occasionally to prevent the parasites from becoming resistant to them. Here, a paste wormer is being administered by syringe.

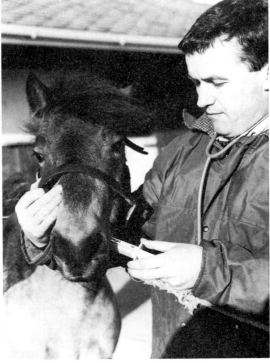

If your horse or pony does not have a current vaccination certificate arrange for him to be vaccinated *immediately* against tetanus and against equine influenza (*see* pages 81 and 83). At the same time, get your vet to check whether his teeth need rasping. Natural wear results in the outside edges of the upper molars and the inside edges of the lower molars becoming sharp and often causing sores on the cheeks or tongue. The horse becomes reluctant to accept the bit and may have difficulty in eating properly. Horses' teeth continue to grow throughout their lives, and it is a simple matter to rasp off the sharp edges and make the horse or pony more comfortable.

Check the condition of your horse or pony's shoes and book an appointment with your farrier at an appropriate time. If you want years of good service from your horse or pony, never neglect his feet – they have to carry him and you! Good shoeing is essential. The feet must be properly balanced by

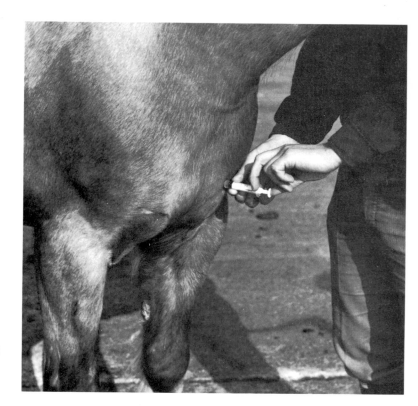

All horses and ponies should be routinely vaccinated against tetanus and equine influenza.

Rasping the teeth removes the discomfort of sharp edges caused by uneven wear, which can cause cheek ulcers, prevent proper mastication of food and cause the horse or pony to resist the bit.

skilled trimming and the right size shoe fitted, well supported at the heels, with the toe neither left too long, nor rasped away to meet the shoe in front (dumping).

If your new arrival is going to share his pasture with others, it is advisable to keep him in for the first week to avoid the possibility of passing on any infection or illness. Otherwise, he can be turned out after two days, once his wormer has taken effect. He will probably set off to explore his new surroundings, then, having made a circuit or two of the field to assure himself that it is a safe place, he will have a roll and settle down to grazing. Obviously, you should keep an eye on him until he is grazing happily.

Horses will sort out their own hierarchy when turned out together, by challenge and counter-challenge (pulling faces, squealing and threatening to kick), but usually without resorting to actual physical violence. Occasionally a particularly dominant or jealous horse may bully another, especially if a third horse is introduced to two others who are used to each other's company. In this case, if they don't settle down within a couple of days, the troublemaker will have to be separated from the others. Come out of the field once you have turned your new arrival out with strangers, but do not leave until you are satisfied that all is well.

The easiest way to manage your new horse or pony is to work out a daily routine and stick to it. For jobs that have to be done less frequently, keep a diary and note ahead the things that need to be done on a monthly, or once or twice yearly basis. The diary can be as simple or as comprehensive as you like and can include everything from shoeing and routine vet's visits to field and stable maintenace (*see* opposite). You might also find it useful to keep a record of any changes in your feeding regime and your fitness training programme, if you are training for competitions.

APRIL

Monday 2 Schooling at home. Dobbin not responsive enough in his transitions – must tell instructor on Thursday. Turned him out rest of day. Started to increase concentrates to build up to competition level. 'X-brand' wormer given.

Tuesday 3 Farrier visit – he advised a biotin supplement to try to improve the condition of Dobbin's hooves. Hacked out one hour, walking and trotting – new shoes OK.

Wednesday 4 Bought biotin supplement and started adding recommended dose to feed. Went to common to do fast work before breakfast, then turned him out. Weather fine and his fitness is improving. Spent evening picking up droppings from field.

Thursday 5 Evening lesson at local school: concentrating on accurate figures and transitions for Saturday's competition. Some improvement, but we need to work at it.

Friday 6 Ten minutes schooling then short hack. Cleaned and checked tack and loaded horsebox for tomorrow.

Saturday 7 Our first event at the local riding club! We had a stop on the cross country (my fault for not having enough confidence), but a clear round show jumping. The least said about the dressage the better – but we'll learn!

Sunday 8 We both deserve a rest day.

A daily diary

What is the most efficient method of daily management for your horse or pony? This will depend mainly upon your own circumstances, but the best rule of thumb is to keep him in the most natural conditions possible, whilst paying proper attention to his health and well-being. This means that if you have enough grazing, your horse or pony can live outside for most of the time, perhaps wearing a New Zealand rug in winter if necessary. When you get to know your horse better you will be able to tell from his condition and his behaviour whether it is necessary to bring him in. Show horses are usually stabled from the New Year and rugged up to help bring their summer coats through early. Your horse will also have to be stabled for longer periods if you are short of grazing space, but be sure to make up for this with ample exercise.

In summer, if the weather is hot, horses are often brought in during the day to give them shelter from the sun and the flies, (although a large shady area in the field will serve the same purpose), and turned out to graze at night when it is cooler.

It is not difficult to organize a daily stable routine to fit in with your other commitments, such as school or work and as an example, we will look at the routine for a horse who is stabled at night and turned out during the day. This is known as the combined method of management and includes all the basic elements of looking after a horse or pony.

Your programme should look some thing like this:

ROUTINE TASKS

Daily tasks
Feed; muck out stable; groom and check horse for health and injuries; exercise; strap horse on return (optional); wash bit and wipe down tack.

Weekly tasks
Collect droppings from field; check water supply; check for rubbish etc. thrown into field by strangers; buy in feed as required; completely clean tack and check for damage.

Monthly tasks
Book regular farrier's visit; worm every six weeks approximately.

Yearly tasks
Routine vet's visit for tetanus and equine influenza booster vaccinations and teeth check/ rasp. Carry out field and pasture maintenance – hedging, fencing repairs, harrowing, reseeding, fertilizing, rolling, weed control. Order hay and straw for winter. In spring, clean and repair winter rugs. Horsebox/trailer maintenance (every six months).

Stabled horses and ponies are usually anxious for their morning feed and the tasks of mucking out and grooming are easier if you can feed first, perhaps before your own breakfast, or while you are doing other jobs around the yard.

How much you feed your horse will depend upon how much work he is doing as well as his type, breed and size. The total amount of food he consumes will hardly vary. The proportion of concentrates to bulk though, will change. When a horse or pony is at grass and not working, he needs mostly bulk food to keep his digestive system working properly, to maintain his bodyweight and condition and to keep him warm. As he begins to work and becomes fitter, he will need a greater proportion of energy-giving concentrates.

A New Zealand rug in winter saves energy by helping to keep the horse warm and also prevents the problem of rainscald. It must be carefully fitted to avoid rubbing, particularly at the withers and shoulders.

RULES TO REMEMBER

- Fresh, clean water should always be available but if your horse has emptied his bucket when you go out to feed him in the morning, offer him a drink before feeding.
- Good feeding should always depend upon quality rather than quantity.
- Avoid feeding your horse or pony immediately before or after exercise. His digestive system won't function efficiently if his stomach is full of food when he is working and after work he needs time to relax before eating.
- The horse's digestive system is designed to work continuously, so allow for this in planning your feeding regime. If he is out in his field all day, obviously he will graze, but if he is stabled most of the time, smaller, more frequent feeds are preferable to two large ones. Give the largest feed at night.
- Make any changes to your horse's feeding regime gradually to avoid upsetting the delicate balance of bacteria which enables his digestive system to function properly.
- Always keep the increase of exercise in your fitness training programme ahead of the increase in the proportion of concentrates in the horse's diet.
- Always decrease concentrates before you decrease exercise and cut them down immediately if your horse has to be off work for any reason. A horse on a high energy diet, who is not using up the energy in work may be prone to 'tying up' (azoturia – *see* page 79), as soon as exercise is resumed.

If the horse is going out for the day, he can have his rugs changed and be turned out before you muck out, making the job easier still. If he is to stay in, it is safer and easier for the beginner to tie him up using a quick release knot (*see* illustration over).

WHAT YOU NEED FOR MUCKING OUT

Have your equipment (a fork, broom, wheelbarrow, skip or manure basket and rubber gloves if you wish) ready outside the

Quick release knot.

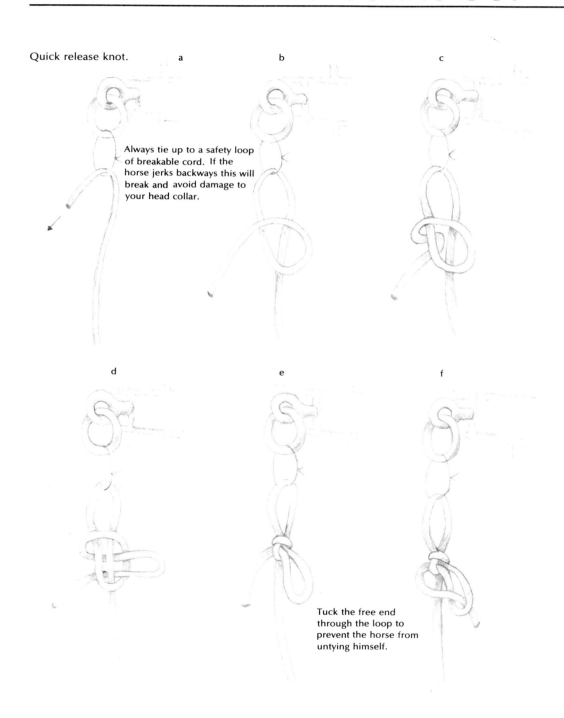

a

b

c

Always tie up to a safety loop of breakable cord. If the horse jerks backways this will break and avoid damage to your head collar.

d

e

f

Tuck the free end through the loop to prevent the horse from untying himself.

door before you start. With the horse tied up, the door can be left partly open and the muck transferred directly to the wheelbarrow if used. Otherwise, it must first be piled against the door and then transferred, to avoid any possibility of the horse escaping. A plastic or sacking skip, however, can safely be brought into the stable. If you want to use a fork, obtain one with blunt prongs. Serious accidents can occur if a horse suddenly takes fright and leaps on to a sharp pronged hay fork.

First, remove all droppings and wet or soiled bedding, whether this is straw, woodshavings, shredded paper or peat. Pile up the remaining clean bedding in one corner, then thoroughly sweep out the stable to remove all debris. Allow the floor to dry before re-laying the clean bedding, either for the day if the horse is staying in, or later on, if he is going out until evening.

Stables must be well mucked out every day and allowed to dry before the bed is relaid.

Some horses may be obliging enough to put their noses into a headcollar if directly approached with the noseband held open in front of them, but a more effective and horsemanlike method is to approach the horse at his shoulder – the way friendly horses approach each other – then slip the headcollar on by passing your right hand, with the headstrap under his chin, up and over the far side of his poll, whilst slipping the noseband over his nose with your left hand (assuming you have approached the left side of the horse). Then fasten the buckle.

Catch your horse without using titbits if possible, but if you have a horse or pony who is difficult to catch, show him the titbit, but don't actually let him take it until you have secured him by passing the leadrope high up around his neck and holding it under his chin. Most horses won't struggle when caught in this way.

Stand to the horse's side when putting on the headcollar.

The horse should be trained to walk forward alongside his handler, who has a firm hold of the lead rope under his chin, with the slack safely looped and carried in her left hand. Never wind a leadrope around your hand.

To lead your horse or pony take the leadrope firmly in your right hand (if you are on his left or 'near' side), about 6in (15cm) from the end, with the slack loosely taken up in your left hand. Never wrap the leadrope around your hand – should the horse or pony take fright and bolt, you could be dragged along and injured. Say 'Walk on', firmly and walk ahead without looking back. A well-trained horse or pony will walk willingly beside you, but a schooling whip in your left hand with which you can reach behind to tap the horse's flank, will encourage him if he is reluctant. This method is also used for teaching untrained youngsters to lead.

When turning your horse or pony out into his field again, always turn him to face the gate and make him stand as you remove his headcollar. You are then out of harm's way if he leaps away in excitement.

Why does your horse need to be groomed? The most basic reasons are to clean off excessive mud so that he can be tacked up, and to improve his appearance. A horse at grass, who is not being ridden for long periods, needs no grooming other than to see that he does not develop problems such as mud fever and rainscald. The natural oils secreted by the skin will protect him from the rigours of hard weather.

Before exercise, all that is needed is to brush off any mud with a dandy brush (use a body brush for the head), and to pick out the feet. As you groom, check the horse over for any minor injuries and problems with feet or shoes.

Thorough grooming (strapping) should be reserved for rugged and stabled horses and ponies, since it strips the natural protection from the coat. It also stimulates the circulation and removes dirt and sweat from the coat of the ridden horse, keeping the pores of the skin open and healthy, and helping to prevent sores caused by pressure and rubs from tack. Therefore it should be embarked upon after exercise, when the horse is warmed up and will obtain the greatest benefit.

Begin with a body brush, using short, firm, circular strokes in the direction of the hair growth. Every few strokes, clean the body brush by drawing it across a rubber curry comb. 'Banging' is a traditional method of stimulating the circulation and

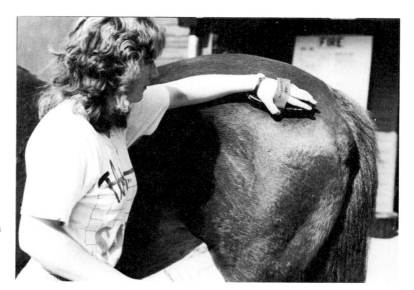

The body brush is used with a firm, circular motion and is cleaned every few strokes with the metal curry comb, held in the other hand.

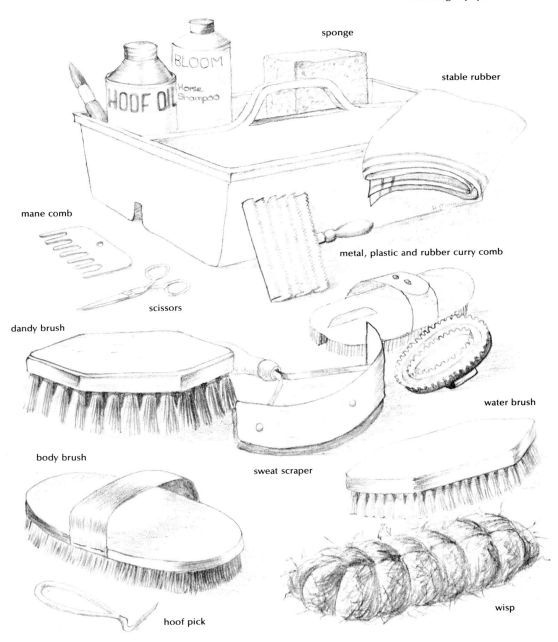

Grooming equipment.

sponge

stable rubber

mane comb

metal, plastic and rubber curry comb

scissors

dandy brush

water brush

body brush

sweat scraper

hoof pick

wisp

Using a body brush, showing circular strokes following lie of hair.

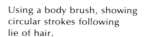

Using the curry comb to clean the body brush.

Lifting and picking out the forefoot.

Lifting and picking out the hindfoot.

Tap the curry comb on the floor so that scurf and dirt falls out.

Some basic grooming techniques.

Feet should be picked out daily, before and after riding, the hoofpick used towards the toe.

helping to build up the muscles of show and competition horses. A special leather pad or a hand-made 'wisp' of straw is used on the muscle areas of the neck, shoulders and quarters, using a rhythmic 'banging' and massaging motion. Never 'bang' other areas of the body, especially the sensitive loins.

The body brush is also used to tidy up the mane and tail – being soft it does not break the long hairs. The mane is shortened and thinned by 'pulling' a few hairs at a time. The same method is used to tidy the top of the tail at the dock, although the tail is often left full and then plaited for competitions (*see* above). Some breeds, however, traditionally have their manes and tails left full and flowing.

Bathing your horse or pony is unnecessary, unless you particularly want to for a special occasion. Use an equine shampoo that will not irritate the horse's skin, rinse the lather off well and make sure that he dries off quickly without catching cold afterwards, lungeing him if necessary.

To pick up your horse's near forefoot, stand at his left shoulder facing his rear. Slide your left hand down the back of his leg to the fetlock and ask him to pick up the foot. A well trained horse will respond automatically. If he does not, lean against his shoulder and repeat the command. Pick out the foot from the heel towards the toe, cleaning all the debris from the sole and clefts of the frog. Many preparations to preserve and promote the growth of the hooves are available, but their main value is as a moisture barrier, either to help keep the wet out or to prevent feet drying out, which is an especial danger in stabled horses or in dry weather. (An appropriate biotin supplement is more likely to improve poor feet than any external preparation and you should ask the advice of your vet or farrier.)

Divide the hair at the top of the dock into three sections (1, 2 and 3 above). Pass the first strand over the third strand, then the third over the second, taking up a little more hair as you go. Continue plaiting, taking up more hair with each turn and keeping the whole as neat and tight as possible. On reaching the end of the dock, continue plaiting to the end of the strands, which are then secured with a needle and thread. The plait can then be turned under and stitched in a loop with the loose ends tucked away and secured.

Once groomed, your horse or pony can have his turnout rug put on and go out to his field. When he comes in for the night, his stable should be prepared for him, with a good bed laid, fresh water in his bucket and his feed and haynet ready. It will be easier to change his rugs before giving him his feed.

LAYING A BED

Bedding for the night should be laid thickly enough to provide a warm bed, without the horse treading through it to the floor and should be banked up at the sides for warmth and safety.

A good, deep straw bed with the sides banked up for comfort and safety.

Good quality long oat straw makes excellent bedding but is seldom available nowadays. Avoid dusty straw at all costs – the spores from poor quality hay and straw are one of the commonest causes of ill health and impaired fitness in horses and ponies. Woodshavings are the most inexpensive and readily available alternative. They form an excellent warm bed and are economical to use, either in pre-packed form (including a 'dust-free' standard) or obtained loose from timber merchants. If you buy any shavings that have not been specially packaged for horses, always check carefully for any foreign bodies, such as nails or other sharp objects, when laying down new shavings. When mucking out, the shavings to be retained should be thrown against the stable wall to break up clumps and provide aeration.

Shredded paper is favoured by those who need a completely dust-free environment. It does however compact easily and all soiled paper must be removed every day to prevent the smell of ammonia fumes. Moss peat is less readily available, but provides a good bed when efficiently managed.

RUGGING AND BANDAGING

Many owners nowadays use fitted under-rugs for extra warmth, but if you use a blanket, it should be placed well forward, up the horse's neck, then slid back into position so that the coat hair lies flat.

Stable bandages are only necessary for therapeutic reasons, following injury or after strenuous competitive work. Don't be tempted to use them as a matter of routine. Unless your horse or pony is very tired, it is better to let him relax naturally after hard work and to keep his legs cool. Wet bandaging is of no practical value (the water soon warms up), so if cold treatment is needed either hose the legs or use a proprietary cold pack. Bandages must always be carefully fitted, to avoid uneven pressure which disrupts circulation to the limbs.

Do not forget to have a final check to see that your horse or pony is comfortable and settled last thing at night, especially if he has worked hard during the day. Replenish his water if it has run out, give him his final feed if required, and his last haynet.

Leather is still the traditional material for harness making and is expected for showing and most competitive uses. However, now many useful and practical synthetic materials are finding acceptance for everyday use and in competitions, such as driving marathons and endurance riding, where practicality is more important than presentation. The main criterion is to see that your equipment is safe, be it leather or synthetic.

Tack must also fit the horse or pony correctly, to avoid rubbing and pinching, sore backs and withers and girth galls. Keep your tack clean and in good condition to aid your own safety and help avoid these problems.

Leather tack should be taken apart at least once a week and cleaned with a damp sponge and saddle soap, then buffed with a dry cloth, paying special attention to buckle tabs and girth straps. Occasional application of a proprietary leather preserver will also keep leather supple and waterproof and help to prolong its life. Bits and stirrups should be rinsed clean and dried to prevent rust spots. They can be polished for special occasions, but don't polish the mouthpiece of your horse's bit.

What tack do you need? A new horse or pony may be purchased complete with his tack, or you may need to assemble a set from scratch. A snaffle bridle with a simple jointed bit is most frequently used and unless you know that your horse or

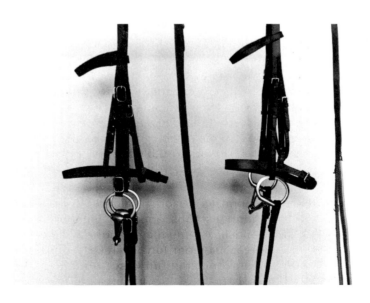

Traditional leather snaffle bridle (*right*) and webbing bridle. Synthetic tack is very practical and increasingly popular.

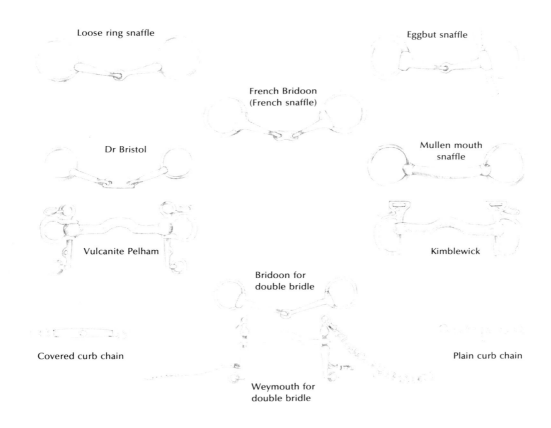

Loose ring snaffle

Eggbut snaffle

French Bridoon
(French snaffle)

Dr Bristol

Mullen mouth
snaffle

Vulcanite Pelham

Kimblewick

Bridoon for
double bridle

Covered curb chain

Plain curb chain

Weymouth for
double bridle

Commonly used bits.

pony goes better in something else, this is the best starting point. Alternative bits can be fitted to the basic snaffle bridle (*see* above).

Snaffle bits can be either jointed or unjointed, the most commonly recommended being a single jointed thick mouthpiece with either eggbut or wire rings. This type of bit acts upon the lips, the tongue and the bars of the mouth and is generally considered to be milder than curb bits which act more strongly upon the jaw and the poll. However, there is much truth in the adage 'There are no severe bits, only severe riders' and the strongest curb bit, in sympathetic hands, is far kinder – and more effective – than the mildest snaffle in heavy, incompetent hands. If you have difficulty in achieving a harmonious partnership with your horse or pony, think about having some lessons together, before you think about trying yet another different bit.

The double bridle has an extra piece of leather, the sliphead, to hold a second bit. The two bits used in a double bridle are the curb and the bridoon, which is a thin snaffle. The curb may have a mullen mouthpiece or a 'port', with cheeks of varying length. The longer the cheeks and the higher the port, the more severe the potential of the bit. The bridoon lies above the curb in the horse's mouth and the purpose of the double bridle is to give the rider greater precision in giving the rein aids.

The snaffle bridle is ideally fitted with a simple cavesson noseband. A drop noseband is useful for a horse who evades the bit by opening his mouth or by getting his tongue over the mouthpiece. The drop noseband will also bring pressure to bear on the nose if a horse is reluctant to respond to the rein aids. A flash noseband prevents a horse from opening his mouth and crossing his jaw, but does not exert the same pressure as the drop noseband. A grakle or figure 8, which is a crossed noseband, does exert pressure on the nose, but allows more freedom of the jaw, and thus it is useful for horses who are inclined to gallop on too strongly.

Plain leather reins can be varied by numerous patterns – plaited, rubber covered and continental webbing with leather stops are all popular variations.

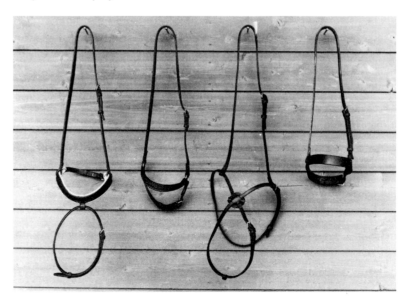

Commonly used nosebands (*left to right*): flash, drop noseband, grakle or figure 8 and cavesson.

Cavesson and double bridle.

Types of Saddle:

1. General purpose
2. Dressage
3. Jumping
4. Dual purpose eventing
5. Endurance
6. Showing
7. Racing

Saddles are made according to the purpose for which they are required to be used, such as dressage, jumping, endurance riding or racing. However, if you want a saddle which can be used for all purposes, the compromise 'general purpose' saddle is the one to buy. It must fit both you and your horse.

Whatever the type of saddle, the 'tree' must be of the right width to give a clear channel through the 'gullet' from front to back, but must not be so narrow that the withers are pinched. The length of the saddle is another important consideration, particularly with short-backed horses and ponies where a saddle which is too big will press on the loins. Never buy a saddle which is too big for a pony on the grounds that it could still be used for the next pony when the child has grown. A saddle which fits can be sold on with the pony, whilst one which does not fit properly will cause sores and probably won't fit the next pony either.

So far as the rider is concerned, the seat (measured from the stud at the side of the pommel to the centre of the cantle), must be large enough to accommodate the rider comfortably, but not so large that he slides backwards and forwards in it. The flap also needs to be long enough to fall below the top of the rider's boot, although this is usually only a problem for very tall riders.

Many saddle features can be varied as required. A dressage saddle, for example, will have a deep seat and recessed stirrup bars. The flap will be straight cut to show off the horse's scope for movement, the rider with a 'long' leg. A showing saddle will be small and light, covering as little of the horse as possible, whilst still affording a secure seat. The flap will be straight (for hacks), or slightly forward (for hunters), and the seat will be fairly flat, to detract as little as possible from the natural line of the horse's back.

A jumping saddle will have a flattish seat, to allow the rider to slide backwards whilst jumping and will have a forward cut flap, usually with substantial knee rolls. Saddles can be custom-made to incorporate any of these features. Dual purpose eventing saddles combine a deep seat with a forward cut flap and knee rolls.

Stirrup leathers should be of good quality and of the right length to be adjusted several holes in either direction. Poor quality leather stretches easily. It is important to check the stitching on your stirrup leathers regularly. Stirrups should be

Parts of the saddle.

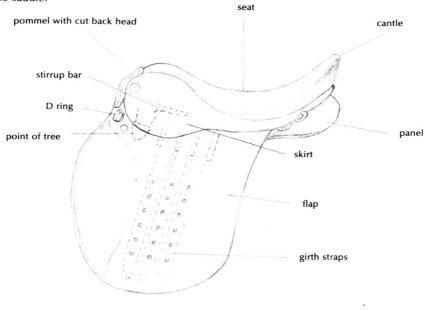

pommel with cut back head

seat

cantle

stirrup bar

D ring

point of tree

skirt

panel

flap

girth straps

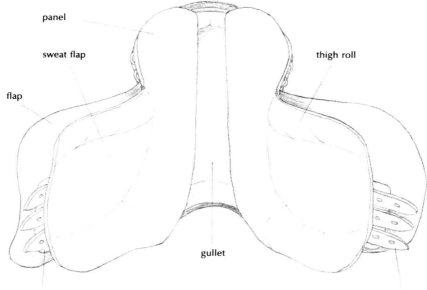

panel

sweat flap

thigh roll

flap

gullet

buckle guard

girth straps

Types of saddle (*left to right*): dressage saddle, general purpose saddle and jumping saddle.

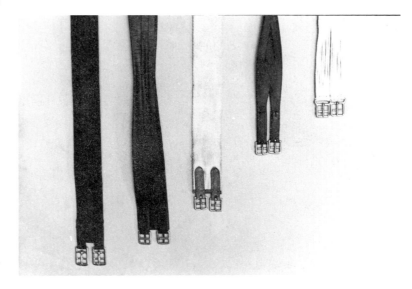

Types of girth (*left to right*): foam padded cotton girth, padded leather girth, lampwick girth, Balding girth, nylon string girth.

the right size (with a quarter of an inch to spare on either side of your boot when correctly placed in the stirrup). If they are too large, it will be difficult to maintain a good position; if too small, there is a danger of your foot becoming trapped should you fall.

Girths are made in many different materials and which you choose is a matter of practicality and personal preference. The most practical everyday girth available at the moment is the foam padded cotton type, which is comfortable for the horse and fairly easy to wash. Lampwick is also comfortable, if cleaned regularly, and string girths are inexpensive but care should be taken to see that they do not pinch. Leather girths never lose their popularity, either the folded type, or the shaped 'Balding' girth. These should be cleaned and treated with leather preservative regularly to keep them soft and supple.

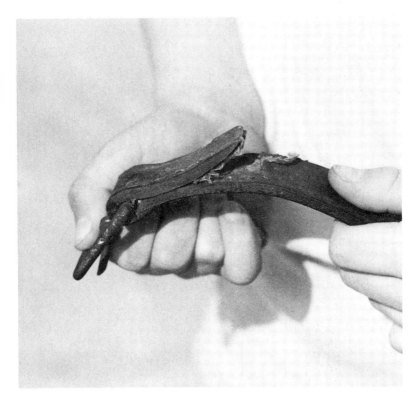

Check stirrup leathers and girths regularly for worn stitching.

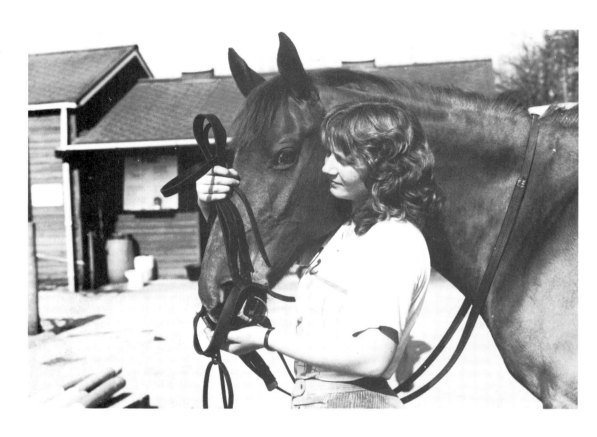

Putting on a bridle. The noseband could also be held up out of the way of the bit.

To put on your horse or pony's bridle, stand at the near side and put the reins over his head. They can then be used to restrain him should he move when the headcollar is removed. Take off his headcollar. Take the bridle in your right hand and the bit in your left with the noseband lifted out of the way. Slip your right hand under the horse's chin and over his nose, which can be held gently whilst you insert the bit into his mouth. Slide your thumb between the bars of his mouth if he does not immediately open it to receive the bit. Avoid banging the bit against his teeth. Lift the headpiece and slip it over his ears, first the off-side, then the near-side, taking care not to rub the bridle against his eyes. Fasten the throat-latch (allowing four fingers' width between throatlatch and cheekbone), then the noseband (allowing two fingers' width between noseband and jaw). The noseband should lie just above the bit, but below the cheekbones. A snaffle bit should be fitted at such a height that the horse's lips are just wrinkled. If a curb bit is used, the chain should come into play when the cheeks reach an angle of 45 degrees from the vertical and the links must lie flat against the chin groove. A lip strap should be used to keep the chain in position.

Numnahs or saddle pads should be put on well forward and slid back-into position so that the coat hairs lie flat. They should be pulled well up into the channel of the saddle to avoid any pressure on the horse's spine. The saddle, with the stirrups run up and the girth folded over the seat, should be lowered gently on to the horse's back, not dropped into place with a bang. Be sure that the numnah is smoothly in place before loosely fastening the girth. Do up the girth by degrees, to give the horse a chance to become accustomed to its tightness, finally tightening it just before you mount.

Putting on a saddle. The handler is placing the saddle well forward to slide it into position. The horse has turned his head to see what is happening, but is relaxed and confident that his handler will not bang the saddle down on his back.

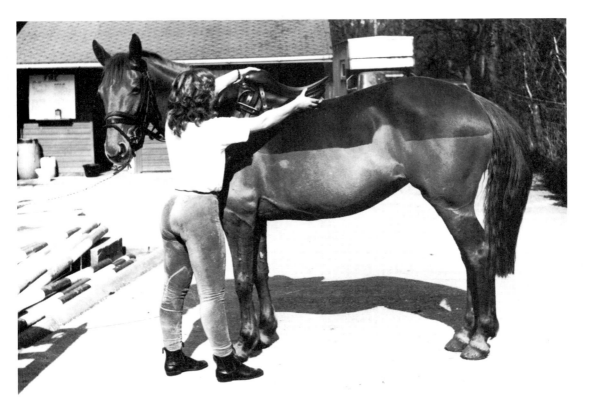

The basic tack of saddle and bridle is all you should need for a well-schooled horse or pony. There may be times when additional equipment will be useful, but do not make the mistake of attempting to substitute 'gadgets' for adequate schooling. They should be looked upon as aids to improvement, not means of control and prevention.

Martingales, for example, only come into effect when a horse is disobedient, or perhaps, excitable. By preventing him from raising his head to evade the bit, the margingale enables the rider to maintain a positive influence through the aids. However, if it is fitted so tightly that it restricts the horse's movement unnaturally, the effect will be to prevent correct work, with the horse being unbalanced and leaning on it. A running martingale (which attaches to the reins) is more frequently used than a standing martingale (which attaches to the noseband and does not allow sufficient scope for the horse's head and neck to stretch when jumping).

Many other schooling aids can be used for training young horses and re-schooling older horses. The Market Harborough, for example is designed on the same principles as the martingale, but it acts on the bit. The *chambon* and the *de gogue* martingale take these principles further, by acting also upon the poll. Draw reins act directly upon the bit to prevent the horse raising his head. All these schooling aids should be treated with respect and expert advice must be sought before they are used. In inexperienced hands, they will create problems, not cure them.

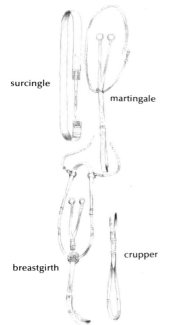

surcingle

martingale

breastgirth

crupper

ADDITIONAL TACK

There are some additional items of tack you may need, concerned with safety rather than schooling. A crupper is a strap which attaches to the rear of the saddle, with a padded leather loop through which the tail is passed. Its purpose is to prevent the saddle from slipping forward on ponies and horses with flat, rounded withers and when going down steep hills. A breastplate, either the hunting or racing type, is used to prevent the saddle from slipping backwards, when going up steep hills or when jumping. A surcingle, usually elasticated, is used over the top of the saddle and is an insurance against the girth breaking during cross-country riding or racing.

During competitions and for schooling, vulnerable legs may need protection. Bandages offer the most support and are recommended for schooling young horses. Exercise bandages should always be smoothly applied over gamgee or cottons, to prevent uneven pressure. Taping them will provide extra security during competitions.

Boots are available in many materials, shapes and forms. Look for those made of impact resistant material, which also mould to the shape of the horse's legs. Boots or bandages should always be worn when lungeing, to avoid injury from the horse brushing, or striking into himself.

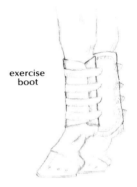

exercise boot

Horse rugs fall into three categories – those for use when the horse is turned out, those for use in the stable and those used during competitions.

The turnout or 'New Zealand' rug used to be a straightforward blanket-lined canvas or flax waterproof garment fastened at the chest, with either crossed surcingles or a single surcingle and hind leg straps. Nowadays, however, there are many more sophisticated designs and materials available, but the main criterion for choice should be that the rug should fit your horse or pony properly. This means it should not press on his spine or withers nor should it rub the points of his shoulders, and it should slide back into position after a buck and gallop or a roll.

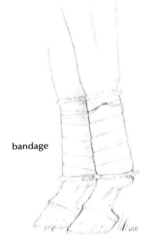

bandage

Stable rug design is less crucial, since the horse is less likely to indulge in violent activity whilst stabled. The main criteria for stable rugs is warmth and durability and again there is a wide choice of materials and designs. The traditional stable rug is wool-lined jute, usually used with an underblanket and fastened with a padded surcingle.

The main purpose of rugs used during competitions is to allow the horse to cool off, whilst avoiding the possibility of catching a chill. The traditional 'cooler' is the anti-sweat 'string vest', but it should be recognized that this is of no value unless used under a blanket or day rug, the whole purpose being to trap warm air and allow the moisture to evaporate without the horse becoming cold. Many modern 'breathable' synthetics are now available which do the job efficiently.

Horses often sweat up when travelling and can easily become chilled, especially on a long, tiring journey, so it is advisable to provide suitable rugs, according to the weather and the ventilation of the transport vehicle.

Legs should be protected from knocks and from the possibility of self-inflicted injury whilst travelling. All in one travelling boots cover the legs from above the knees and hocks to the heels. If bandages are used, separate knee and hock boots are necessary, whilst overreach boots are a sensible precaution, especially for horses travelling for the first time. Tail protection

Fitting travelling or stable bandages. The bandage should always be unrolled from the inside towards the outside of the leg. The padding reduces any risk of uneven pressure and in the case of travelling bandages also provides protection to the heels. The bandage is brought down below the fetlock and back up to be fastened neatly on the outside. Tapes should be tucked under a fold of bandage to prevent them from coming undone.

is essential for horses who are inclined to lean back, as their tails can soon be rubbed raw. A tail bandage helps keep the tail neat but is insufficient if protection against rubbing is needed, when a sturdy tail guard of leather or tough synthetic fabric should be used. A poll guard is recommended for horses who are likely to throw their heads up when being loaded.

A neatly fitted tail bandage, with tapes tied at the back where the knot will not rub. It is usual to turn a fold of bandage down over the knot. The tail guard is attached to a surcingle and fits over the tail bandage for extra protection should the horse rub his tail whilst travelling.

The person who keeps his horse as a weekend hobby may look out of the window on a Saturday, see it is a sunny morning and decide to 'go for a ride'. The competitive rider, however, sees every ride as part of a planned programme that involves riding the horse five or six days a week.

The grass-kept part-bred horse or native pony can cope quite happily with weekend hacking, provided he is otherwise well looked after. However, he cannot be expected to hunt or compete.

There are three basic components to fitness training, all essential and complementing each other. School work on the flat is aimed at improving the horse's ability to carry the rider in balance, increasing his suppleness and muscle strength and thereby reducing the likelihood of stress induced injury. Steady work over longer distances increases stamina, or endurance ability, by improving the horse's capacity to utilize oxygen in producing energy and also toughens up limbs, joints and muscles. Fast work is the final aspect of fitness training and should be limited to the last phase before a competition, after the horse has achieved the basic level of fitness required.

Fitness should always be part of a planned programme.

The best way to plan your horse's fitness training is to write it down and then to keep a diary of what you actually do, so that you can see how close you are to achieving your objectives. First ask yourself 'What do I want to get my horse fit to do?' Is it hunting, eventing, showing, jumping, or distance riding? Each activity requires a different emphasis in the horse's training. For example, suppose you are planning to tackle a riding club event.

SAMPLE TRAINING PROGRAMME

Aim: Riding Club one-day event in six weeks' time.

Needs:
To improve dressage. Basic schooling is adequate for every day riding, but practice in riding a formal dressage test is needed.
To gain more confidence across country and learn how to tackle specific types of fence.
To improve suppleness for show jumping.
To increase general fitness.

Suggested weekly training programme:
Day 1 – Following rest day, start the week with an hour's steady exercise, walking and trotting, preferably up and down hills.
Day 2 – Dressage, cross country or gymnastic jumping lesson.
Day 3 – 1½ to 2 hours steady exercise, including steady cantering where possible and jumping any safe natural obstacles encountered on ride.
Day 4 – 1 to 1½ hours exercise and intoducing fast work/interval training, which should build up in intensity as training progresses; or ¾ hour schooling session at home, depending on progress and stage of training.
Day 5 – Another dressage or jumping lesson if possible. Otherwise schooling at home.
Day 6 – Short schooling session, followed by relaxing hack.
Day 7 – Rest day.

Items to include in a daily training diary:
Type of training: e.g. cross country session, tackling drop fences and water jumps.
Duration of exercise.
Terrain/location.
Weather conditions.
Note about performance: e.g. sweated up, keen and interested, jumped well, etc.
Heart rate data: a) during exercise if using a heart monitor b) recovery details post exercise (e.g. heart rate 42 beats per minute, ten minutes after end of exercise).
Management details, i.e. time turned out, time in stable.
Accidents, injuries and other interruptions to the training plan.
Quantities and type of food, including any supplements.
Farrier's visits.
Vet's visits.
Any changes in routine.
Journeys and travel details.
Competition details.

Every horse or pony needs a basic level of schooling to make him a safe, well-mannered ride. This is his early education, which should have been thoroughly taught before he is sold on to the novice or beginner rider. Throughout his life, this basic level needs to be maintained and built upon, or its benefits will simply be lost. Horses and ponies quickly learn bad habits and, if good behaviour and the correct way of going are not continually reinforced by practice and training, misunderstandings will soon occur, and the unfortunate horse or pony will be labelled 'difficult' or 'a problem horse'.

It is therefore essential for the future success of the horse/rider relationship that the new owner understands what basic schooling entails, why it is necessary and how to progress afterwards. This is impossible without expert, practical help and is why you should take your new horse or pony for some lessons at an approved riding centre, preferably before the problems begin.

Schooling is a basic part of fitness training, suppling up muscles and improving balance.

The horse or pony's initial training is all about balance. The equine may look as though he is ideally designed to carry a rider, but it does not take much thought to realize that he actually evolved to carry his own body, with most of the weight slung beneath his back. In riding him, we require him to alter his natural ability and carry weight positioned vertically above his back. It should be obvious firstly that this requires an adjustment of the horse's own centre of gravity from a lower, forward position to a higher, further back position and, secondly, that for the horse to accurately move as the rider wishes, the rider must remain in perfect, co-ordinated balance with the horse. The instant the rider loses precise, controlled balance, the horse also cannot help becoming unbalanced, strive as he might to co-operate. This is why it takes a skilled rider to give the horse or pony his initial training.

The adjustment of the horse's balance, and the development of his musculature to maintain it, is achieved mainly by work on a circle, initially by lungeing without a rider on his back and,

Lungeing is a valuable skill, which it is worth taking the trouble to learn. This horse appears calm, but the handler should wear gloves, as a lunge line dragged through the hands can cause a nasty burn.

A fit, healthy pony.

progressively, with a rider and by riding circles and other 'school figures'. The process to reach a basic level where the horse is said to be ready to be 'ridden on' takes several months, but the dedicated rider will seek continual improvement throughout the horse's active life, asking progressively for the more advanced movements collectively known as 'dressage'.

The novice rider's job, on acquiring his horse or pony, is simply to maintain what the horse or pony already knows and to avoid making mistakes. After this he can begin to progress in whatever sphere appeals to him. The mistake that many beginners make is to assume that they have bought a horse or pony who is 'trained' and that therefore no further training is required. Detailed advice on schooling is beyond the scope of this book, but a schooling session even once a week, with knowledgeable help, will make all the difference to the pleasure you will gain from your riding.

A horse correctly tacked up for lungeing, with lungeing cavesson over
a snaffle bridle, plain side reins, roller and breast girth, plus
brushing boots and over-reach boots.

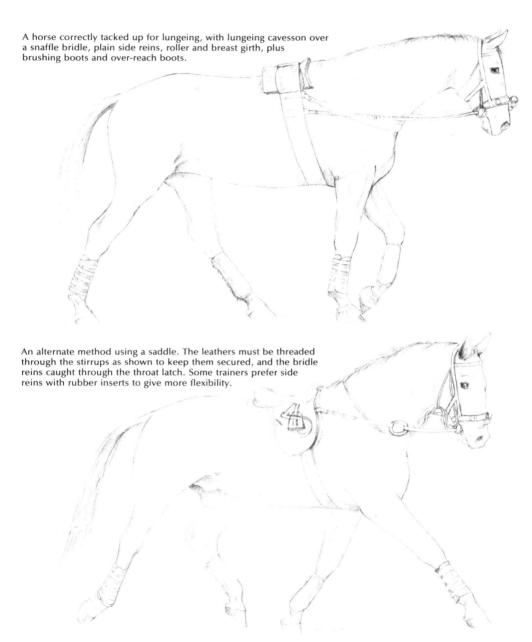

An alternate method using a saddle. The leathers must be threaded
through the stirrups as shown to keep them secured, and the bridle
reins caught through the throat latch. Some trainers prefer side
reins with rubber inserts to give more flexibility.

Lungeing equipment.

Roadwork and plenty of walking should be continued throughout fitness training.

Fitness can be defined as the physical and mental ability to give a successful performance in a given discipline at a given level. In addition to the physical exercise imposed, attention must be paid to the horse's general health, his diet and his mental well-being.

The object of fitness training is to improve the horse or pony's ability to produce energy and use it in athletic performance. All the body systems are involved.

Fitness training is a continuous process which can be divided into two distinct stages: basic training which applies to all, and specialized training for a specific purpose.

Basic training begins with the horse or pony who has been roughed off and kept at grass, but is now required to work. It is now recognized that sudden changes of routine are detrimental and can cause problems such as colic, so when a horse or pony is first brought up from grass his new diet should be introduced gradually. Soaked sugar beet pulp has a slightly laxative effect and so is an excellent mixer for concentrates when they are first introduced and, indeed, for any stabled horse or pony. Make sure plenty of clean, fresh water is available in the stable and turn the horse or pony out for part of the day.

Work should begin with walking exercise for twenty minutes to half an hour per day, increasing to an hour over the first week. By the end of two weeks, slow, steady trotting can be intoduced, preferably uphill. Lungeing for short periods will also help to improve suppleness – ask an expert to show you how it is done. After a month, slow canter work can be introduced and mounted schooling should begin. At the end of six weeks the horse or pony should be approaching a basic level of fitness and be ready to move on to more intensive work. Through all fitness training, continue with as much steady walking, up- and downhill, as possible. This is the most beneficial method of building up strong ligaments, tendons, joints and muscles, with the least danger of injury.

Many horses and ponies dislike water at first, so crossing streams should be included in training.

Increased fitness is achieved by progressively imposing controlled amounts of 'stress', to encourage the body systems to increase their capacity for energy production and become more efficient. Three methods are used – working faster, working more frequently and working for longer periods.

Fast work is extremely strenuous and you must be careful not to overtax your horse or pony's resources. A half-mile gallop twice a week in the final fortnight before a competition should be plenty. Alternatively, 'interval training' is an excellent and more scientific method of using fast work to get your horse fit. This involves cantering or trotting alternated with walking, in various combinations of a few minutes at a time, on a repetitive basis, allowing the horse or pony a chance to recover between each short burst of intensive work. Programmes need to be worked out individually.

How often you work your horse or pony will affect the rate at which his fitness increases. Daily work (with one day off a week) is essential and in some circumstances, for example schooling for dressage or show jumping, it may be more beneficial to give the horse two shorter sessions a day, rather than one long one. In this way, he has time to digest what he has learned and is less likely to become bored or stale.

Duration of work is the third factor involved in fitness training and it is long, slow, steady work which improves the horse's stamina and capacity for endurance.

Variety keeps your horse or pony alert and interested. Most enjoy jumping, once properly taught.

Preparing horses and ponies for showing requires a rather different approach than for performance work, since much more emphasis is placed on appearance. However, travelling to shows and putting on a good performance in the ring is more strenuous than it might seem and a good basic level of fitness is needed.

CONDITION

The horse or pony must also appear in good condition, with a gleaming, healthy summer coat and be expertly turned out, so preparation for the summer shows begins after Christmas, when show horses and ponies are stabled and rugged, to encourage early shedding of the winter coat. A good broad spectrum supplement will ensure that all essential vitamins and minerals are supplied, while in Britain boiled linseed jelly is commonly added to encourage an extra shine to the coat.

Unfortunately show horses and ponies are frequently over-fed to achieve 'show condition', with many resultant ailments such as laminitis and joint problems. Fortunately, the various

Stages of plaiting. The hair is first divided into an odd number of even bunches (seven is traditional); neat plaits are then made and secured with a needle and thread or elastic band. The plait is then turned under twice and secured. Sewn plaits look neater and stay in better for the show ring.

show authorities are beginning to take notice of this unhealthy fashion and it is to be hoped that fewer 'fat' animals will be seen in the show ring in future.

GROOMING

The show horse or pony must be impeccably groomed, with his mane and tail plaited (except for certain specific breeds – check your breed society rules). Show animals are frequently bathed, though with a really fit, thoroughly groomed animal this should not be necessary and daily 'strapping' should achieve a shining coat as well as toned-up muscles. The mane and tail, however, will need to be shampooed and the mane pulled to an appropriate length for plaiting. A tail which is to be plaited must not be pulled, but tails may be neatly pulled to

Pulling the mane. The mane is brushed free of tangles then, using a comb to separate the hair, the longer underneath hairs are pulled out, a few at a time, with the fingers. Manes should be pulled regularly, a little at a time, not all at once.

show off the quarters, as an alternative to plaiting. Tails are usually trimmed straight across the bottom to fall just below the hocks when carried naturally. Some breeds, for example Arabs and British native ponies are shown with manes and tails full and free flowing, neither plaited nor pulled, but simply tidied up sufficiently to create the best appearance for the ring.

Heels can be neatly trimmed with comb and scissors, but the practice of trimming whiskers, which are a sensory organ and the hair from the inside of the ears, which keeps out dust and flies, is to be discouraged.

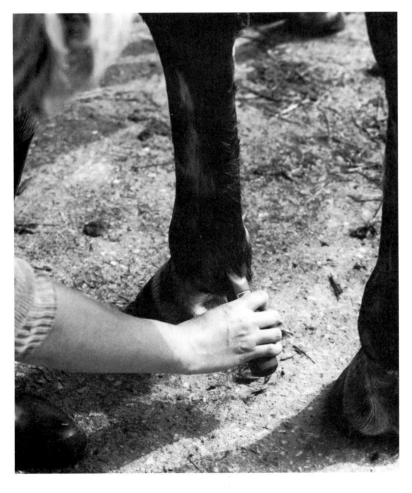

Heels can be neatened by careful trimming with clippers or scissors against the direction of hair growth.

Vital Figures

Resting heart rate
  Regular and 32–48
  beats per minute

Respiration
  6–18 full breaths per
  minute

Temperature
  99.5°–101.5°F

When you go down to your stable early in the morning and your horse is looking out to greet you, ears pricked and looking for his breakfast, you know he is basically healthy and well. Equally, if he trots or gallops around his field with head and tail in the air, throwing in the odd buck for sheer fun and exuberance, there cannot be much wrong with him.

What other signs show that your horse or pony is healthy and in good condition?

Some are obvious. Look for a shining, flat coat that gleams even if not groomed for a show; for alert, clear eyes, pricked ears and clean, dry nostrils. You should also look for clean, cold legs and hard, well-shaped feet with resilient horn.

Other aspects of the healthy horse or pony are less obvious. For example, the mucous membranes of his eyes and mouth and his gums should be salmon pink, showing a healthy blood supply. His normal resting heart rate (pulse) should be regular and between thirty-two and forty-eight beats per minute, with ponies having slightly faster heart rates than horses. His respiration rate (breathing) should be in the range of six to eighteen full breaths per minute and his temperature between 99.5° and 101.5°F (37.5° and 38.6°C).

Every owner should be able to check these health signs for himself. The easiest way to take the horse's heart rate is with a stethoscope and if you are planning to do much competitive riding, monitoring the heart rate is a good way to check the horse's progress towards fitness. The fitter the horse becomes the less time it takes for his heart rate to recover to normal following exercise and in most situations this should occur within thirty minutes. The stethoscope is placed on the near side, just behind the elbow and the two-phase 'luub-dup' sound counts as one beat. The pulse can also be taken by feel, with the fingers, at various pulse points, most easily at the large vein under the cheek bone, but also at the withers or on the legs.

Respiration is counted by observing the rise and fall of the flanks at each complete breath. This is quite easy with a quiet horse at rest, but is always more difficult with a hot horse after exercise, when the flank movement may easily be confused by panting.

Taking the temperature requires a little more care – ask your vet to show you. The thermometer should be shaken down to

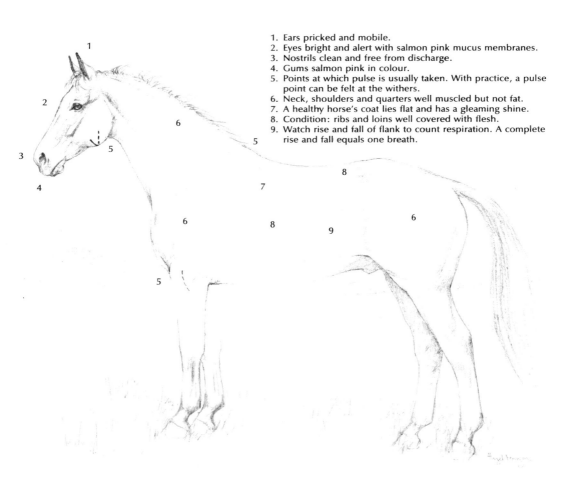

1. Ears pricked and mobile.
2. Eyes bright and alert with salmon pink mucus membranes.
3. Nostrils clean and free from discharge.
4. Gums salmon pink in colour.
5. Points at which pulse is usually taken. With practice, a pulse point can be felt at the withers.
6. Neck, shoulders and quarters well muscled but not fat.
7. A healthy horse's coat lies flat and has a gleaming shine.
8. Condition: ribs and loins well covered with flesh.
9. Watch rise and fall of flank to count respiration. A complete rise and fall equals one breath.

well below 100°F (37.7°C) and greased with vaseline or suitable medical lubricant. With the handler standing well to one side to avoid any risk of being kicked, he inserts the thermometer gently, making sure it touches the wall of the horse's rectum. The thermometer is held in place for one minute, then removed and read.

Learn to notice your horse or pony's condition and to spot the gradual changes that may occur.

Signs of a healthy horse.

Signs of Ill Health:

1. Dullness/listlessness
2. Loss of appetite
3. High temperature
4. Discoloured mucous membranes
5. Abnormal respiration
6. Pain
7. Staring coat
8. Abnormal droppings or urine

Signs of illness include a dull eye, lack of energy and enthusiasm, and loss of appetite. The horse may churn up his bedding due to restlessness during the night, or he may stand listlessly in a corner, his head hung low. His mucous membranes may be discoloured red or yellowish; there may be a discharge from eyes or nostrils and he may have a high temperature. Respiration may be laboured or noisy. The healthy horse makes no sound when breathing, except for a rhythmic exhalation at the canter, or the 'high blowing' characteristic of highly bred horses.

Breaking out into patchy sweat, pawing the ground and swinging the head round to the flanks are all signs of pain. The horse may also roll, but this is not to be confused with the normal healthy roll in the dust that the horse enjoys when turned out in the field.

SKIN

The skin of a horse in good health will be loose and elastic. If it is stretched and taut, causing the coat hairs to stand up instead of lying flat (known as a 'staring' coat), there is something wrong.

DROPPINGS

A healthy horse's droppings are moist, smooth and firm and his urine is a clear, pale colour. Loose 'cowpat' droppings or hard dry ones are a sign of digestive trouble, while dark, clouded urine may indicate more serious problems.

The following is a brief description of the most common equine ailments. For full information on diagnosis and treatment the reader is referred to 'Your Horse's Health' (*see* Further Reading).

AZOTURIA

Otherwise known as 'Monday morning disease', this causes much alarm due to its sudden, dramatic onset, with symptoms of sweating, pain and stiffness in the large muscles of the hind quarters. The horse should be kept warm and moved as little as possible until the vet arrives. This often occurs when a horse has been rested without a reduction in hard feed and is then returned to work.

BONE PROBLEMS

Curb: A swelling at the back of the hock due to strain. Early lameness should disappear although the swelling may remain.
Ringbone: A bony enlargement due to damage at pastern or coffin joints. The seriousness depends on the actual site of damage and may result in permanent lameness.
Sesamoiditis: Damage to the sesamoid bone at the back of the fetlock, due to strain and often resulting in chronic lameness.
Spavin: Bony swelling inside the lower hock joint, resulting from damage caused by strain. Lameness occurs until joint has fused. (*Bog Spavin*: Soft swelling of hock, due to poor conformation, trauma, or possible mineral imbalance. Unlikely to cause lameness.)
Splint: A very common stress injury in young horses. Tearing of the ligment connecting the splint bone to the cannon bone causes a swelling which is at first soft, then bony. Initial lameness usually disappears once bony growth has stabilized and the splint will often reduce in size.

COLIC

Abdominal pain due to various causes, commonly the blocking of an artery by worm larvae, or a sudden intake of unsuitable

Curb

Splint

A capped hock.

food. The horse shows obvious signs of pain, sweating, biting or kicking at the flanks and rolling. Contrary to common belief, a twisted gut, which may occur in some types of colic, is not caused by rolling. Do not walk the horse, but keep him as quiet and warm as possible and call the vet, since an accurate diagnosis of the cause is essential.

FILLED LEGS

Commonly associated with the morning after a hard day's work, the traditional remedy was overnight bandaging. This is not recommended as a dependency will develop. May also occur in horses brought up from grass. Exercise quickly disperses the build up of fluid which causes the 'filling'.

LAMINITIS

Primarily caused by a change in diet involving excessive carbohydrate intake (e.g. too much fresh spring grass) which

The laminitic stance.

upsets the balance of bacteria in the gut and allows endotoxins into the bloodstream. One effect is to constrict the peripheral blood vessels, particularly those supplying the sensitive laminae of the feet. These die, causing inflammation, pain and damage to the structure of the foot. Immediate medical treatment, within hours of the first signs, is often successful. Otherwise drastic surgical treatment, with protracted intensive nursing, will be necessary.

LYMPHANGITIS

Infection of the lymphatic system causing painful swelling. Veterinary treatment is essential.

NAVICULAR DISEASE

Mistakenly believed to be incurable, this degeneration of the navicular bone in the foot can be treated in several ways. The use of the vaso-dilatory drug isoxsuprine has proved successful, as has surgical treatment and further research is currently taking place.

RESPIRATORY PROBLEMS

Influenza: The ubiquitous 'virus' is feared by all horse owners. In fact there are several infectious respiratory diseases, the most common being equine influenza. It is simple good management to vaccinate against this extremely infectious disease and there is no excuse for neglecting to do so. Should a horse or pony contract the disease, complete rest and isolation are essential.

SAD (Small airway disease) or Heaves: The allergic reaction to dust and spores in hay and straw which causes coughing and loss of performance. The provision of a dust-free environment will cure the condition.

Strangles: A common bacterial infection causing a sore throat, high temperature and thick nasal discharge, with the formation of an abcess on the glands between the jaws. Recovery begins once the abcess has burst, but good nursing is required to clear up the condition satisfactorily.

SAND CRACKS (OR GRASS CRACKS)

These occur in the hoof wall due to poor foot care (i.e. infrequent trimming), and are exacerbated by dry conditions. Various forms of treatment are employed to halt the progress of the crack and regular attention is needed for the six months or more until the crack grows out.

Sand crack.

SKIN PROBLEMS

Lice: Occasional infestations affect horses and ponies, usually when kept in poor conditions. Dousing with louse powder provides the remedy.

Mud Fever: Caused by bacteria which thrive in wet conditions. The affected area should be kept clean and dry, the scabs gently groomed away and mild antiseptic applied. Antibiotics may be prescribed in severe cases.

Rainscald: Similar to mud fever and usually occurs on the saddle area.

Ringworm: Common infection caused by fungi, producing groups of round scabs. Extremely contagious, also infecting humans and so protective clothing should be worn and all equipment thoroughly disinfected. Equipment used for the infected horse should not be used for others. Treat with antibiotics, prescribed by your vet.

Sweet Itch: Irritation caused by midge bites resulting in intense rubbing of mane and tail until hair is lost and skin inflamed. Various treatments available to discourage midges and reduce damage, but most successful solution is to keep horse in during early morning and late afternoon when midge activity is at its height.

TENDON STRAIN

Strained or ruptured tendons usually occur suddenly during hard work. The immediate application of ice will control the swelling and anti-inflammatory drugs are also used. Complete rest is required until the condition has stabilized, followed by carefully controlled exercise. The traditional treatment of 'firing' causes unnecessary further damage and pain to the horse, requiring a long period off work while healing takes place and it leaves permanent scars.

TETANUS

Caused by bacterial spores which enter the blood through wounds or possibly via the stomach producing a toxin which causes progressive paralysis and death. All horses should be vaccinated against this still common bacteria. The condition is deeply distressing and nearly always fatal.

URTICARIA

Widespread, weal-like swellings which suddenly appear due to an allergic reaction, either to food or other substance absorbed by the horse's system. Antihistamine treatment is effective, but the source must be identified to prevent further outbreaks.

WARTS AND OTHER TUMOURS

A difficult area of treatment since surgical removal often encourages regrowth or further growth in other areas of the body. Simple warts may disappear of their own accord. The most common dangerous tumours, however, are the malignant melanomas found only in grey horses, which may stay unchanged for years, but are ultimately fatal.

The first aid box should include: antiseptic or antibiotic wound dressing or powder; cotton wool; gauze dressings; poultice dressing; three or four 4in (10cm) wide elastic bandages; scissors; and sticky tape (safer than safety pins). Proprietary hock and knee bandages are also useful, if rather expensive.

Every horse owner occasionally has to deal with minor injuries and wounds. It is sensible to keep an adequately stocked first aid kit immediately to hand in the stable.

There is no need to panic at the first sight of blood – a considerable amount can be lost before the situation becomes dangerous. However, each incident must be quickly assessed and the appropriate action taken. In most cases, bleeding stops quite quickly, but if bleeding is severe a pressure bandage should be applied *around* the wound area.

Simple bruising is best treated with frequent applications of ice, or cold hosing. Ice must not be applied next to the skin, but over gamgee or a bandage.

Puncture wounds are frequently missed when they first occur, usually in the foot. The trouble begins when the horse goes lame due to infection and the build up of pus. The wound must be kept open to allow drainage and should be poulticed for two or three days with a suitable dressing. Antibiotics may be prescribed.

Lacerated or incised wounds should be cleaned with a mild antiseptic once bleeding is reduced and then dressed with antibiotic spray. Bandaging is usually unnecessary for minor wounds. Larger wounds require stitching and this should be done immediately for effective healing. Always call the vet for wounds involving joints, other deep wounds and those where foreign matter has penetrated deeply.

There are some basic rules for coping with accidents and injuries:

1. Assess the situation calmly and decide whether veterinary attention is necessary.
2. Do not delay the treatment of any problem. If you are unsure what to do, the vet should be consulted.
3. Follow veterinary advice and instructions precisely. Ask questions if you are uncertain what is required.
4. Keep a close eye on your horse or pony's progress and watch out for signs of infection or worsening of any condition. Again, consult the vet.
5. Pay attention to stable hygiene. Keep food bowls and utensils clean; disinfect rugs, blankets, grooming kit and even the stable following any infectious disease. Don't forget your own boots.

Of all the things you can do to get to know your horse or pony better, there is one more valuable than anything else and that is to spend *time* with him. Whether riding him, grooming him, teaching him lessons from the ground or simply sitting on the paddock fence watching him, hours spent in his company will teach you more than any book or outside influence. A good instructor may show you the finer points of riding and a horsemaster the practicalities of horse and pony care, but really understanding your horse or pony must come from within yourself and from slowly building up his trust and confidence in you. This is not something achieved in the first week or two of ownership, but over years of shared activities and mutual companionship.

A horse or pony who is handled firmly but kindly will invariably obey, to the best of his ability and understanding, without question. Excessive force, however, will be met with resistance and if he does not understand what is required the horse will become progressively confused and uncertain until he has no choice but to refuse to co-operate and eventually to challenge the handler's domination. In extreme cases he may try to get away from the handler or react aggressively due to fear. This is when many inexperienced horse owners find themselves in difficulty.

Horses and ponies live naturally in the social environment of the herd, which is why it is a kindness to provide your own equine with the companionship of others of his kind. To the domesticated horse or pony however, his human handler becomes his herd leader, who must play the dominant role.

A pony in full winter coat. You should avoid using barbed wire in the paddock.

Be aware that your horse or pony sees the world from an equine viewpoint and not from a human viewpoint. He learns by example and repetition; he can show considerable intelligence in reacting to any current situation, but cannot reason about what may happen tomorrow.

His physiology also means that he has a different perspective on the world from humans. Raising and lowering his head changes the range of his sight, but he has blind spots directly in front and behind him. This is why you should always approach your horse at his shoulder and speak to him if you are moving to his rear.

The horse's bifocal vision.

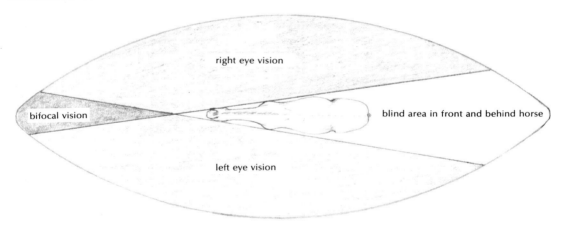

right eye vision

bifocal vision

blind area in front and behind horse

left eye vision

His ears, as well as showing different moods can swivel to hear sounds from different directions. A healthy horse's ears are continually moving, unless he is asleep. His mouth also, may have a taut or wrinkled 'worried' expression, or be soft and relaxed.

Understanding all these things can help you in handling your horse with ease and remember also that your mood will communicate itself to the horse. If you are calm, relaxed and unhurried, the chances are that the horse will be calm and relaxed. If you are tense and nervous, making sudden, jerky movements, the horse will think there is something to worry about. The more your horse or pony trusts you, the more confidence he will have that whatever you ask him to do is safe and the less distracted he will be by outside influences. This is essential if you want him to pay attention to *you* when you are out together and not to everything else that is happening around him.

Familiarization with strange situations takes time. For instance, if you want to do well in the show ring, you should take your horse or pony to a few shows without any idea of winning, or even going into a class, just to introduce him to the noisy, colourful environment. He will soon decide that he has 'seen it all before' and settle down for you to concentrate on his performance.

Two young riders enjoying a canter.

Few private horse or pony owners are lucky enough to have the regular use of an indoor school, arena jumps, cross country fences, or extensive gallops. It is a matter of seeing what is available and making the most of that.

A corner of a field can be turned into a suitable schooling area without too much difficulty, for use when the ground is relatively dry. If possible, fence the area off, so that it is at least enclosed. This will make schooling safer and help to improve the horse's concentration as he will be aware of the confines of his immediate environment. Choose a level area that drains well. Putting down a ring of stable waste, either straw or shavings, will help preserve the ground surface.

A little imagination can contrive schooling jumps from lumber that you may have available, bearing in mind a few safety rules. Poles must be thick and solid, as thin ones snap too easily and may injure a horse. Old horseshoes can be adapted by a friendly blacksmith to make cups and these must always be fitted on the landing side of the fence. Old car wheels, filled with concrete and with an upright bedded in the hub, make cheap home-made wings.

In winter, schooling at home becomes more difficult, with the risk of poaching the ground, and injury to the horse or pony schooling on wet, sticky going. Try to continue training by booking some time at the nearest riding centre. Most will hire out their arenas and this is worthwhile if you can persuade one or two friends to join you.

Many people use hunting as a way of obtaining cross country riding in winter. If this does not appeal, find your nearest course and book some schooling rounds in spring and autumn.

Hacking out or exercising should not be a chore. Much useful schooling can be achieved on quiet country lanes and bridleways. Ride your horse or pony efficiently, concentrating on maintaining a good position and keeping him balanced. Make frequent transitions and try to make them precise; practise lengthening and shortening the stride and leg yielding. Vary your routes as much as possible and use every available hill for fitness training. Get to know your horse's paces and time him over measured distances. The countryside is full of gates, so learn how to open and shut them efficiently from the back of your horse. Small natural obstacles, such as ditches and logs, can be jumped, once you have checked the safety of the landing side.

Home-made jumps.

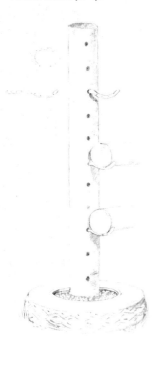

Home-made jumps are fun, but follow basic safety precautions. This jump is not safe as the pole is firmly wired to the tree and will not collapse if the pony hits the jump.

The horse should learn to perform a turn on the forehand while the rider opens and closes a gate.

Where is all this training going to take you?

There are riding clubs and the Pony Club where you can find a wide range of activities and much friendly competition and helpful advice. In other countries there are also clubs and riding centres where enthusiasts can get together to improve their skills.

The horse owner who rides for personal pleasure and owns a good 'all round' type of horse or pony has no need to specialize. Many people participate in everything from show jumping to long distance riding and there are competitions available to suit every level.

The minority sports also have their own enthusiastic followers, whether for carriage driving, western riding, side saddle, mounted games or vaulting. Even polo, once considered the preserve of the wealthy, is a growing sport at local club level.

Those keen on improving their horsemanship can study for numerous tests to prove their skills, for example the British Riding Clubs' grade tests or Pony Club tests.

Whatever direction you take, the fascination of horses is endless. As has often been said before 'The more you know, the more you find there is to know.'

Action The way in which a horse or pony moves. This varies among breeds, e.g. the high knee action of the Welsh Cob. A 'true' or 'faulty' action describes efficiency of movement. Examples of faulty action are a) Dishing: horse swings leg out to side and b) Plaiting: horse swings feet inwards and places one in front of the other.

At grass The horse is turned out night and day and is resting or not in full work.

Bulk food Food comprising a high proportion of roughage, e.g. grass or hay.

Canter One of the four paces of the horse. A gait with a three-time beat in which the sequence of leg movements when cantering to the left is 1) off hind, 2) opposite diagonal pair (i.e. near hind and off fore together), 3) near fore (referred to as the 'leading leg'). Vice versa when cantering to the right.

Cob A weight-carrying type of horse, with compact, muscular conformation and short legs. Also 'Welsh Cob', one of the British native breeds.

Combined management A system of keeping the horse stabled part of the time and out of doors part of the time (usually in at night and out during the day, or vice versa in hot summer weather).

Concentrates High energy food, e.g. oats, barley, proprietary compounds, etc.

Condition The physical status of a horse, e.g. poor condition, show condition, 'carrying too much/not enough condition'.

Conformation The physical structure of a horse and how it fits together. Good conformation is essential for athletic performance.

Crib biting Catching hold of a solid object such as the edge of the manger with teeth, leading to wearing. Also usually associated with windsucking.

Dressage The training from basic schooling through to 'high school' or advanced movements. This also refers to competitive riding to show the horse's gymnastic ability and responsiveness on the flat.

Filled legs Swelling of the lower legs due to inactivity. It often occurs the morning after strenuous activity, or when a horse is first brought in from grass.

Gallop The fastest pace of the horse, with a four-time beat.

Hacking Riding out for pleasure.

Hand The traditional method of measurement for horses. Originally the width of a hand, but standardized to 4in (10cm).

Heart rate The parameter by which fitness is most easily assessed. Normal range is 36–42 beats per minute, increasing to over 200 beats per minute during fast fitness training.

High blowing Snorting exhalation of air through the nose when cantering. Characteristic of Thoroughbreds and highly bred horses.

Leg yielding Lateral movement in response to seat and leg aids, with the horse's head bent away from the direction of travel.

Lungeing Working the horse or pony on a circle, controlled with a long line and lunge whip. Used in basic training of horse and rider and to exercise older horses when riding is not appropriate. Also used at start of any fitness programme as a suppling exercise.

New Zealand rug Turnout rug used to keep horses warm and dry in winter. Traditionally made of flax lined with wool, but often canvas and now synthetic materials are often used.

Numnah or saddle pad Shaped pad used under saddle to reduce jarring on horse's back. Does *not* compensate for an ill-fitting saddle.

Paces The four gaits of the horse: walk, trot, canter and gallop.

Pony Equine traditionally under 14.2 hands high. Show classes for show hunter and working hunter ponies now include animals up to 15 hands high.

Port An arch in the mouthpiece of some bits, e.g. Kimblewick, ported pelham, or Weymouth. The higher the port the more severe the action of the bit.

Poultice An agent used to draw impurities and pus from wounds. It may have a traditional base, such as bran, or more usually now be a proprietary poultice.

School figures (or movements) Set patterns used in schooling horses, e.g. circles, serpentines, diagonals, etc.

School work (or flatwork) Training the horse in dressage movements, to increase suppleness and muscular strength.

Spur Artificial aid, used by expert riders to give precise leg aids. *Not* a goad.

Temperament The horse's mental attitude and response to being handled and ridden.

Thoroughbred The racing breed of horse developed from crossing three imported oriental stallions with indigenous mares. The breed has been exported all over the world.

Transitions Changes from one pace to another, which should be carried out smoothly and precisely.

Trot The pace between walk and canter, comprising the alternate movement of diagonal pairs of legs in a two-time beat.

Vices Behavioural problems including biting, kicking and rearing; or stable problems such as crib biting, wind-sucking and weaving.

Walk The slowest pace, with a four-time beat in the sequence off hind, off fore, near hind, near fore.

Warmblood A breed developed by crossing hot blooded (e.g. Thoroughbred) horses with cold blooded (e.g. draught) horses. Very popular for dressage work as they combine powerful movement with an equable temperament.

Warranty The guarantee given by a vendor selling a horse at public auction that the horse is sound in wind, limb and eye.

Weaving A stable vice comprising standing at the stable door and swinging the head from side to side, sometimes shifting from one forefoot to the other in the process. Often caused by unsatisfactory lifestyle.

Whip An artificial aid, used to encourage the horse's responsiveness to the natural aids of weight, leg and hand, *not* as a punishment.

Wind-sucking A further development of crib biting, in which the horse draws in air whilst holding on to a solid object with his teeth. Results in poor condition, unthriftiness and makes it impossible to get horse fit. Often caused by unsatisfactory lifestyle.

British Horse Society,
British Equestrian Centre,
Stoneleigh,
Kenilworth,
Warwickshire CV8 2LR

Association of British Riding Schools,
Old Brewery Yard,
Penzance,
Cornwall TR18 2SL

**British Show Hack, Cob and Riding
Horse Association,**
Rookwood,
Packington Park,
Meriden,
Warwickshire CV7 7HF

British Show Jumping Association,
British Equestrian Centre,
Stoneleigh,
Kenilworth,
Warwickshire CV8 2LR

Equine Research Station,
Balaton Lodge,
Newmarket,
Suffolk CV8 7PN

Farriers Registration Council,
PO Box 49,
East of England Showground,
Peterborough
Cambridgeshire PE2 OGU

**Horses and Ponies Protection
Association,**
64 Station Road,
Padiham,
Lancashire BB12 8EF

American Farriers Association
4089 Iron Works Pike
Lexington, KY 40511

**Hunters Improvement and National
Light Horse Breeding Society,**
96 High Street,
Edenbridge,
Kent TN8 5AR

Master Saddlers Association,
Easdon,
Lower Icknield Way,
Chinnor,
Oxfordshire OX9 4DZ

National Pony Society,
Brook House,
25 High Street,
Alton,
Hampshire GU34 1AW

Ponies Association of UK,
Chesham House,
Green End Road,
Sawtry,
Huntingdon,
Cambridgeshire PE17 5UY

Riding for the Disabled Association,
Avenue R,
National Agricultural Centre,
Stoneleigh,
Kenilworth,
Warwickshire, CV8 2LY

Royal College of Veterinary Surgeons,
32 Belgrave Square,
London SW1 8QP

Weatherby and Son,
Sanders Road,
Wellingborough,
Northamptonshire NN8 4BX

American Grandprix Association
P.O. Box 495
Wayne, PA 19087

American Horse Council
1700 K St., NW
Suite 300
Washington, DC 20006

American Horse Protection Association
1000 29th St., NW, #T-100
Washington, DC 20007

American Horse Shows Association
220 E. 42nd St.
Suite 409
New York, NY 10017

**American Riding Instructor
Certification Program**
P.O. Box 4076
Mount Holly, NJ 08060

American Veterinary Medical Association
930 Meacham Rd.
Schaumberg, IL 60196

National 4-H Council
7100 Connecticut Ave.
Chevy Chase, MD 20815

**North American Riding For The
Handicapped Association**
P.O. Box 33150
Denver, CO 80233

United States Combined Training Association
292 Bridge St.
South Hamilton, MA 01982

United States Dressage Federation
P.O. Box 80668
Lincoln, NE 68501

United States Pony Clubs
893 Matlock St., #110
West Chester, PA 19382

**United States Professional Horsemen's
Association**
4059 Ironworks Pike
Lexington, KY 40511

United States Equestrian Team
Gladstone, NJ 07934

FURTHER READING

Drummond, M   *The Horse Care and Stable Manual*
Houghton Brown, J and Powell-Smith, V   *Horse and Stable Management*
Langley, G   *Understanding Horses*
Pavord, T and Fisher, R   *The Equine Veterinary Manual*
Practical Horseman   *Practical Horseman's Book of Horsekeeping*
Rees, L   *The Horse's Mind*
Snow, D H and Vogel, C J   *Equine Fitness – The Care and Training of the Athletic Horse*
Vogel, D J   *The Stable Veterinary Handbook*